transform into a multi-media entertainment venue in the evenings and weekends. The Verne theatre of Heureka will be renovated and converted into a planetarium and one-of-a-kind multivision theatre in the Helsinki metropolitan area.

Capable of accommodating up to a thousand dancing couples, the Music and Dance Centre is a project by Niskankoski Oy that would offer a view over the rapids of river Keravanjoki and the park on the river. The center will provide a multi-purpose venue to host conferences, corporate as well as private events adding to the revenue sources towards the sustenance of the complex.

The City of Culture will provide for a 100 room hotel flanked by cafes and restaurants for tourists and visiting groups to Heureka's science labs and programs.

"Culture City of Vantaa will be a real destination, providing a multitude of cultural experiences for more than a million visitors. The core is still Heureka, the Finnish Science Centre, with its highly interactive and motivating exhibitions on science and technology and its educational services. Heureka has started the project and continues to drive it. The whole complex, when ready, will be of international significance and an interesting role model for the field", says Executive Director, Dr. Per-Edvin Persson ■

Credits: JKMM Architects

UNIVERSITÉ CATHOLIQUE:

Louvain Museum

The Catholic University of Louvain (UCL) intends to build a new museum next to the lake of Louvain-la-Neuve in Belgium. The project of a new building next to the lake of Louvain-la-Neuve will offer new opportunities for a true University Museum of Arts and Civilization.

The future two buildings overlook a 17-acre lake connecting the main town square to a large theater complex.

As a token to the national and international reputation of the city, the building is intended to place the University museum among the leading institutions of its kind in Europe, and will have a similar standing to comparable institutions in the world. The new 4000 sq.M. building will be erected in the city center in front of the new Aula Magna.

To maintain unobstructed views between the city center and the lake one of the museum buildings is underground with a lobby, temporary gallery space, 150-seat auditorium, café, and administrative space

The total area of exhibition space in the new museum will be three times larger than its existing facilities. This increase will allow the development of the museum's mandate to be a place for dialogue in a broader sense. Several exhibition areas will be included in the future building expansion plan: an atrium, an area dedicated to the permanent collections organized into

The 115ft. tall twisted sedum covered tower overlooks the town's east-west artery seemingly afloat on a glass 'cliff'. The four-story atrium inside the tower leads to a pedestrian walkway connecting the museum to the town. Photovoltaic cells fixed to the atrium's louvers will power lighting, and a heat pump system linked to the lake by underground ducts will heat the exhibition rooms.

specific areas, and areas that will host temporary exhibitions. In addition, the expanded facilities will include activity areas, an auditorium seating around five hundred, and a waterfront themed bar and dining experience.

The original museum building opened in 1979 at the University of Louvain (UCL : Université catholique de Louvain), eight years after Louvain-la-Neuve was founded. Over the years, many donations have enriched the original collections which have constituted a remarkable heritage of Arts and Civilisations and are exhibited by rotation. This heritage is centred on the most important tendencies in both European and Belgian Art : from engravings by Albrecht Dürer or Rembrandt to Alechinsky's or Delvaux's paintings, and including Gothic or Baroque sculptures. And yet these collections also open vistas to other continents as well with a rich collection of « primal art » (from Africa and Oceania) or an opening on « popular » or « nad've » arts. Through these varied exhibits the hall-mark of which is historical, cultural and social diversity, whole segments of humanity are made present in the very heart of this new city, in the young province of Walloon Brabant. From one exhibition to

another and with the changing presentation of the museum's exhibits, visitors discover a renewed museum with each season. At any time visitors can learn more about the history of civilizations and the diversity of art in the 20th century. Visitors will also come across university students learning their future professions and school children from the area or from further afield, learning and creating art. This is what a contemporary, living, university museum is : a place of life, where exhibits and visitors from all walks of life meet and interact for mutual enrichment ■

Credits: Perkins + Wills Architects

MARITIME CENTER VELLAMO:

Beacon of Cityscape

Kotka's Maritime Centre Vellamo fulfils a visual as well as a strategical function within the cityscape. The figure of the Maritime Centre guides travellers from the heart of the city out to the north-eastern end of the City Terminal and into a harbour of culture. The Maritime Centre is the hallmark of the city's cultural profile. The role of an individual building in determining the direction of a city's overall architectural development is nowadays recognised as a model for city planning. The Maritime Centre is a notable addition to landmarks associated with Kotka both nationally and internationally.

Cornerstone of the Culture Harbour

The Old Harbour, or City Terminal, will soon be transformed into a Culture Harbour. Work in and around the harbour will coexist with spaces designated for pastimes and cultural activities. In addition to events at the Maritime Centre, the surrounding area will take on a more active role for local residents with attractions including a multipurpose arena, a cinema complex, a ferry terminal and a guest marina. As the first of its kind, the international significance of the Maritime Centre affords it a unique role as the functional cornerstone of the downtown area.

Maritime Vision

The title of the proposal to win first prize in the architectural competition to design the Maritime Centre was HYÖKY, 'swell'. References to the sea incorporated in the building's distinctive architecture link the Maritime Centre to the sea in general and to the unique features of the Kymenlaakso region in particular. The abstract image of a large wave, a swell, which dominates the exterior of the building, and the façade, specially designed to capture the glint of the water, combine to create a physical representation of the sea.

Proactive Cityscape

Situated at the end of the planned culture harbour, the roof of the Maritime Centre, the crown of the cityscape, forms a square which will play host to a wide array of different events. A walkway rising gently from the city centre and widening as it reaches the top of the building leads up to the rooftop square. A sloped floor with a staggered performance space, an incline culminating in a steel-glass covering and the square's position high above the surrounding city together create a unique space suitable for all manner of different activities. The outdoor exhibition space and the main entrance, opening out towards both the city centre and the quayside, form a focal point in the ground-level cityscape.

The interior of the Maritime Centre is characterised by the application of timeless architectural concepts. With the help of natural light, spatial layout and the choice of materials, individual spaces come together to form shifting, adaptable, dynamic spatial units. The entrance, the foyer, with its broad staircase, and the elevated, centrally located exhibition hall housing the permanent collection give the interior of the Maritime Centre its distinctive character; together they form a spatial entity fashioned from free-shaped wall faces, a material world dominated by oak-wood surfaces and the expanding nature of the surrounding space.

Functional Guides

The elevated exhibition space housing the permanent collection, shared by both in-house museums, plays a key role in the Maritime Centre. Each museum's exhibition tour can function independently or as part of a larger tour encompassing both exhibitions. A walkway forming both a visual and a physical link between the two museums' exhibition spaces leads out of the shared foyer. The bridges crossing the elevated permanent-exhibition room guide visitors to the main entrances into each individual museum and to doors leading into the spaces housing the numerous visiting collections. The museum shop, a restaurant, seminar and teaching rooms and an auditorium are all situated in and around the main foyer area.

Maximum Adaptability

The rooms housing the numerous visiting exhibitions, as well as those housing each museum's permanent collections, have been specially designed to make them as adaptable as possible. The form, colour scheme and inbuilt technical equipment in each room have been carefully chosen with regard to the varying nature of different exhibition environments. The clearly defined shape and proportions of these rooms, the neutral grey colouring specified on all surfaces and fittings, and the comprehensive lighting, electricity, heating and ventilation system make them suitable for housing a whole host of different museum exhibitions.

Cultural Focal Point

The Maritime Centre is home to two permanent residents: the Maritime Museum of Finland and the Museum of Kymenlaakso. In addition to the two museums, numerous other organisations will be able to take advantage of the Maritime Centre's facilities. The 250-seat auditorium is fully equipped to serve the needs of a variety of different clients. The foyer design, the educational and seminar rooms and the centrally located restaurant together provide all the services necessary for visiting congresses and musical events. An extensive library is situated on the ground floor and is fitted with a separate entrance. In addition to the two in-house museums, the Kotka Maritime Library, administered by the Kymenlaakso University of Applied Sciences, and the Science Library of the University of Helsinki's Kotka Department will also An Intensive Working Environment

The Maritime Centre's workspaces are divided between the ground floor and the second floor of the building. Spaces used for unloading, restoration, exhibition construction, storage and conservation purposes are organised according to function and situated on the ground floor. The museums' shared administrative office spaces are located on the second floor.

Contemporary Structure

In terms of the methods employed in its construction, the Maritime Centre building is a prime example of modern, Finnish structural engineering. The Maritime Centre is primarily built around a column and beam system of reinforced concrete girders. The ground floor consists largely of structural hollow-core slabs, the middle and upper floors of hollow-core slab constructions, while the walkway on the roof is designed as an inverted structure. Steel girders were used in the upper-floor structure of the wide, elevated area. The rooftop square, the covering over the fitted upper floor and the maintenance area is a combination of steel, glass and aluminium. The outer walls are constructed using a lightweight skeleton structure. Sheet-metal cassettes, painted in a variety of different shades, are the primary building material on

the exterior of the building, to which a lattice made of aluminium and pressed-silk glass has been affixed.

Fruit of Collaboration

In 2004 the City of Kotka held an architectural competition to produce a design of the Maritime Centre. A total of 86 design proposals were received. The results of the competition were announced in January 2005. The City of Kotka, the Museum of Kymenlaakso and the Maritime Museum of Finland collaborated to establish the initial parameters for the design work, and have since worked in close association with the chosen architects from spring 2005 to February 2006, by which time all contractual documentation was finalised. The design plan based on the winning proposal, HYÖKY, is founded on close cooperation between developers, clients and designers ■

Credits: Architects Lahdelma & Mahlamäki

CHANGSHA RIVERFRONT CULTURAL CENTER:

Daring the Dragon

Denton Corker Marshall is one of the world's leading design practices. Currently working in Europe, the Middle East, Asia and Australia, the practice has established a reputation for producing dynamic and innovative design solutions. A studio-based practice that has grown internationally, Denton Corker Marshall's body of work constantly explores the fusing of art, architecture and tectonics into a distinctive architectural language.

Denton Corker Marshall's work is characterised by an uncompromising attitude to design quality. The ability to solve complex design problems is the hallmark of practice. From the world's tallest building down to the scale of a coffee cup, the studio's design approach consistently produces highly original solutions.

As architects, the firm operates from a core of planning. Whenever designing projects their objective is to design beyond site and programme to embrace wider environmental and social concerns.

Denton Corker Marshall (DCM) has won numerous commissions to design buildings of international significance, such as the Stonehenge Visitor Centre and Interpretive Museum and the Manchester Civil Justice Centre in the UK, the Australian Embassies in Beijing and Tokyo and The Melbourne Museum.

Their commitment to pursuing excellence in design has been recognised throughout the architectural and design professions. They have received numerous awards from Institutes of Architects in Australia, Asia and Europe. In 1996 John Denton, Bill Corker and Barrie Marshall were jointly awarded the Royal Australian Institute of Architects' most prestigious and highest honour, the Gold Medal.

Their practice has been successful in a substantial number of design competitions. DCM's consistent success can be attributed to its commitment to design orientated outcomes via the design studio model.

The practice was established in Melbourne in 1972 and is run by founding directors John Denton, Bill Corker and Barrie Marshall, together with Stephen Quinlan in London, Budiman Hendropurnomo in Jakarta and Adrian FitzGerald in Melbourne. It also has offices in Sydney and Brisbane. With 120 architects and design staff, the firm utilises advanced communications and is committed to a global presence with completed projects in 20 countries.

Changsha Riverfront Cultural Park

Design Inspiration

Changsha is a city with a long and distinguished culture. It is noted for many famous figures in history including literary masters and important leaders. Mao Zedong studied in Changsha and the famous Yuelu Academy is located within the city area.

As the capital of Hunan Province, Changsha is a regional centre that is rapidly growing, rebuilding and modernising. The DCM proposal draws on China and Changsha's rich history for inspiration. This is interpreted into a forward looking, dynamic Cultural Building designed for the future.

The Setting & Site Planning

The confluence of the Xiang River and Liu Yang River creates a special place in the city for the Riverfront Cultural Park. The site will be viewed not only from the city but also from across water to the north, west and south west. Our proposal sites the major buildings to maximise outlook to the river from not only the buildings but also the parklands. They achieved this by siting the buildings inland to look over first the park and then the river, giving priority to maintaining a continuous park along the river front. Rather than design individual buildings dispersed in the park DCM proposed to combine the Library, Concert Hall and Museum into what appears to be a single structure. This maximized the potential visual impact of the cultural facilities into a stronger, more memorable form.

The Stage 2 Hotel and Convention Centre are adjacent to create their own identity yet form important elements in the total composition.

Cultural Building Concept

DCM proposed a unique dragon-like Cultural Building (the Dragon Building) that twists and turns throughout its park setting. Each of the three main uses, being the Library, Concert Hall and Museum is contained under a single building skin. This links each of these separate elements into a single building mass.

Contained within this overall twisting roof structure, the Library, Concert Hall and Museum are in fact discrete buildings with clearly identifiable front doors. Between each of these cultural buildings the dragon roof forms covered plazas for drop off and pick up points and for use as large covered outdoor performance and gathering spaces.

At the head and tail of the dragon the roof structure kicks up into the air to form a city gateway to the south and river gateway to the northern end.

Symbolism & Identity

The stunning form of the Dragon Building is derived from China's extraordinarily rich culture. For instance it can be likened with a metaphoric sweep of the calligrapher's brush stroke, or the eternal form of the mythical dragon.

It also reflects the unique regional identity of Changsha seen in the curving flow of the majestic Xiang River or the rolling Yuelu Mountains

The Dragon Building, together with the Convention Centre and the 208 metre high landmark Hotel tower, set within the 36 hectare parkland, is bound to become an international icon.

Imagery – Unique Cladding System

The Dragon Building utilises an innovative and unique pattern to create the cladding system. It comprises a repetitive arrangement of metal panels with integral windows in a distinctive layout.

The extraordinary pattern has never been used before in a contemporary architectural building. It is derived from traditional Chinese artefacts such as the triangulated breakup found in windows and walls in historical buildings such as, for example, Prince Gong's Residence in Beijing.

The pattern breaks up the cladding into standardised panels. These are repeated across the surface of the building for ease of manufacture and assembly. While seemingly complex it is actually made up of a limited number of components regularly repeated. This will ensure economy in construction. The lines in the pattern are given a width forming a basket-like weave. Selected elements become strip windows in the facades. Others are coloured metal strips. They are coloured green, yellow, and orange to provide identity to the respective Library, Concert Hall and Museum uses contained within the total dragon structure.

The Dragon Building will become an extraordinary icon of contemporary world architecture. The perspectives show the potential picture post card photographs that could become the image by which Changsha would be known in the world.

Built Area

Museum	$20,400m^2$
Concert Hall	$14,900m^2$
Library	$24,800m^2$
Carparking	$44,400m^2$
Services	$17,000m^2$
Hotel Tower	$70,000m^2$
Convention Centre	$35,000m^2$
Carparking	$28,400m^2$
Services	$143,800m^2$
Total	$265,300m^2$

Dongqianhu International Educational Forum Complex, Ningbo, China

Design Philosophy

Ningbo is a city which is following Shanghai's lead at the forefront of China's economic development.

Dongqianhu, located at the outer perimeter of Ningbo city, has a treasured value due to its stunning scenery and rich traditional culture.

Building an International Educational Forum Complex in this location will make a significant contribution to society and the local community. The integration of the multi-functions of convention centre, exhibition hall, holiday resort, market and tourist entertainment will provide a historical landmark for future generations.

Inspired by this great mission, the design seeks to pursue a distinctive and dramatic architectural work.

- Highlight the integration of internationalisation and localisation

- Enhance the harmony between humans and the natural landscape

- Emphasize the balance between the conflict of creating a distinctive architecture while preserving a relationship with the natural setting

- Providing a venue with an educational soul which will further the discourse on educational practices both in China and internationally.

Design Principles

By carefully considering the natural landscape and local culture, the design seeks to create a modern architecture instead of simply imitating a traditional architectural form. This will capture the dynamic and lively modern atmosphere that is being sent out presently in the tide of China's economic development.

Masterplan Strategies

The moving undulated building form is adopted in the masterplan in which many buildings form a cohesive whole. The elongated buildings in a horizontal dimension against the lakeshore respond to its natural setting while the beauty of modern architecture is conceived from carefully arranging the 'line', 'dot', 'plane' and colour from the artist's palette. The natural site is preserved as much as possible by condensing single buildings into a continuous form. Buildings are orientated around the lake to maximise views and to create a series of visual corridors by carefully organising scenery nodes along the visiting route.

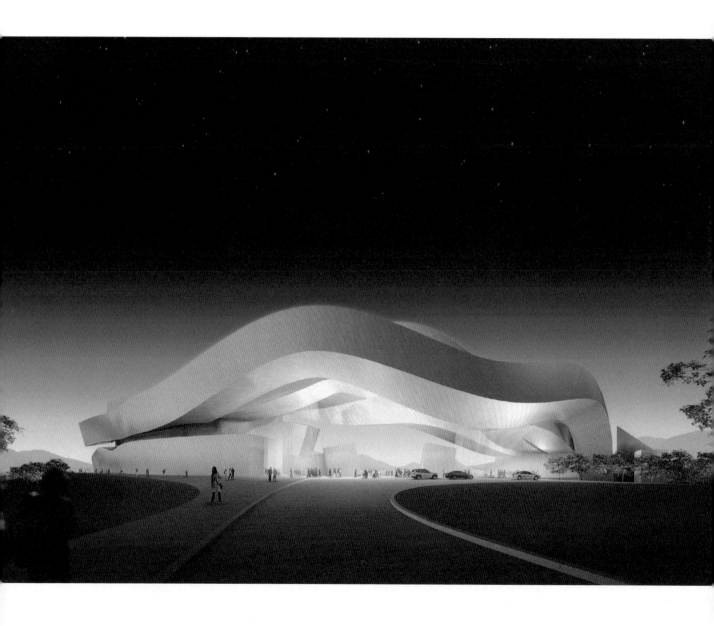

3.5

Building Forms

The design fully considers the natural scenery by creating a long and flowing manmade contour between the line of the lake and the figure of the hills. A floating solid ribbon form is contrasted with the undulating clear glass curtain elevation within the tranquil natural setting like a romantic flowing painting or dancing music notes along a scale of written music. The bold use of the large piece of clear curtain makes part of the building almost disappear in the air and its inverted image unconceived in the water. This has created a formed image of 'four in one' by integrating water, sky, mountain and building into a whole. The rich cultural heritage of the area is portrayed by incorporating abstracted local architectural dialects and vernacular building materials into the design.

The solutions presented in this design are conceived by DCM, inspired by the scenery of Dongqianhu. It has broken the normal rules of architectural design for seeking harmony between human and nature but recognised the same design principles as those masterpieces of architecture in the world. Yet, undoubtedly the design has created a realistic picture in which water, mountain, sky and building are integrated into a whole while a distinctive and dramatic outcome is impressively conceived.

The Setting & Site Planning

The design is conceived as many elements which are linked together by the natural water and mountain landscape. Each element responds to its natural setting in a unique way while at the same time the complex forms a coherent and harmonious whole.

An Island Complex

The forum provides a landmark which faces towards Ningbo city, providing a beacon to guide visitors from the city. A canal has been dug to separate the isthmus into an island, creating an exclusive destination point. As visitors approach they will catch glimpses of the iconic Forum Building, increasing their anticipation and excitement of arrival before the whole complex is revealed to them. The journey can be likened to a scroll painting where elements are revealed a little at a time to gain appreciation of each small section in a sequence before the whole design is revealed.

The forum faces the city as a symbol of education and culture. The hotel and villas faces the lake as a symbol of restoration and harmony. The Forum Building creates a man-made contour between the lake shore and the hills, symbolising rippling water. The terraced form nestles into the landscape. It provides opportunities for meditation and appreciation of the landscape by capturing the best lake views from the site. Every guestroom and public space in the hotel and all living and bedrooms in the villas have their own lake view ■

Credits: Denton Corker Marshall
Reprint: Huseum Design Spring 2006

MUSEUM DEL ACERO:

Transforming an Industrial Relic

Some might have dismissed Blast Furnace No. 3 as an ageing, industrial artifact, but others envisioned a spectacular educational facility—part science center, part museum, part thrill ride—inside its crumbling walls. That dream has finally become a reality. In 2004, Museo del Acero hired AldrichPears Associates, a world-renowned interpretive planning and design firm, to develop the conceptual design and exhibits for the museum. The result is a broad range of unique and engaging experiences, making the Museo del Acero Monterrey's hottest new attraction.

One hundred years ago, Parque Fundidora was the site of the country's first integrated steel mill: Fundidora de Monterrey. After it closed in 1986, the land was reclaimed to provide green space for residents, and educational, recreational, and business facilities for over two million visitors a year. As a National Archeological Industrial Site, the park is already home to a number of beautifully restored heritage buildings.

The entrance to the steel gallery, La Acería.

Dominating the Monterrey skyline, Fundidora's Blast Furnace No. 3 is one of the most recognizable landmarks in the park as well as the city. As a symbol of the importance industry plays in Monterrey's past and future, Blast Furnace No. 3 seemed like the perfect place to provide a fun and educational environment for families and kids to discover steelmaking history, science, and technology. Diego F. Nevárez, Manager of Operations and Visitor Services at the new museum agrees, "What has been for years an icon of our city, is now infused with new life and purpose as a science and technology center."

What makes this museum unique is that it is housed inside the newly restored Horno No. 3. Grimshaw Architects and Oficina de Arquitectura worked with AldrichPears Associates to repurpose the building to meet the needs of a large museum while ensuring the preservation of its historical character. New additions were subtly incorporated into the design. For example, the main gallery was carved out of the large slag pit found adjacent to the blast furnace.

The newly restored Horno No.3.

Steelworkers in front of Horno No.3

Numerous skills were required to round out this international team of designers and producers. One of the highlights of the museum is the multimedia show, El Gigante Dormido, which VISTA Collaborative Arts produced and for which Performance Solutions provided the special effects. The exhibits were fabricated and installed by The Taylor Group, Unified Field developed the computer interactives, Margen Rojo produced the audiovisual materials, and Doug Welch was the lighting designer

Goals and Challenges

The goal of the Museo del Acero is to use steelmaking as a vehicle to get younger visitors interested in science and scientific exploration. The main interpretive objectives are to tell the century-old story of steelmaking in Mexico, explain the process of making steel step by step, and provide visitors with a way of experiencing the excitement of standing next to a working blast furnace spewing molten iron and smoke. The challenge was to figure out how best to tell these complex stories—stories that had never been told before in a museum and science center—in a way that visitors would find fascinating and easy to understand.

Providing visitors with choices

Museo del Acero offers a range of distinct experiences that cater to diverse audiences. Visitors can learn about the history of steelmaking in Mexico in the history gallery, México a Través del Acero; visit the playful, science-based steel gallery, La Acería; see the blast furnace come to life in the special effects show, El Gigante Dormido; or ride the ore lift to the top of the blast furnace to experience El Viaje a la Cima.

Preserving an industrial relic

After assessing the crumbling hulk of Blast Furnace No. 3, the design team made every effort to preserve the historical integrity of the building, and to use it to their advantage. The project was a massive undertaking. Tim Lindsay, Senior Associate and Lead Designer with AldrichPears, comments "the greatest design challenge was the creation of a museum-quality experience within the structure of Horno No. 3—a large and complex industrial artifact. The solution was the careful restoration of the artifact while still permitting public access throughout, and the creation of new, architecturally unique gallery spaces." The entire building had to be stabilized. The cast hall floor—two meters of concrete and steel—was completely replaced. And a special protective coating was applied to all steel structures and machinery to prevent further decay.

Steel gallery, La Acería, is centered around a demonstration stage.

4.1

Historical spaces transport visitors back in time

Today, the furnace itself remains intact. The seventy-meter tall steel structure is now the centerpiece of El Gigante Dormido, a sound and light show that uses music, video, and dramatic lighting to tell the story of Horno 3. Audience members can feel what it was like to be in the presence of an active blast furnace through sound effects, shooting sparks, bursts of flames, and a simulated river of molten iron. The history gallery is housed in what used to be the massive load floor. Beautiful brick columns still line the space and the torpedo car tracks remain visible in the floor. Visitors can ride inside what was once the ore lift to the top of the blast furnace where they can walk along the same catwalks that workers once did. From up high, they can peer down the large throat of the furnace or take in the magnificent views of the site, the city, and beyond.

Engaging the Visitor

The Director of the museum, Luis López Pérez, is particularly thrilled with the many opportunities for hands-on interaction. He notes that, "the Museo del Acero is an invaluable informal learning tool since visitors are really able to relive an industrial process." In the history gallery, visitors can listen to workers' stories on telephones, watch images of steelworkers moving about in a model of Mexico's first skyscraper, and delve deeper into the story of steelmaking through computer interactives. The steel gallery makes use of immersive environments and full body play to transport visitors to the mill or the mine to experience different processes. Kids can slide down a giant cutaway model of a blast furnace or ride an elevator deep into a coal mine. Visitors of all ages can operate a model electric arc furnace, blast for ore in a mine, or design a futuristic vehicle using steel.

The main entrance to Museo Del Acero

A "ribbon" of steel shows visitors the way through the history gallery, México a Través del Acero.
Photo: The Taylor Group

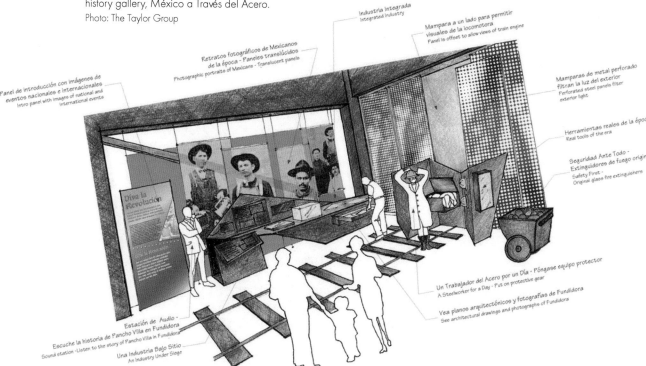

Using icons to anchor spaces

Impressive icons, like a recreated torpedo car and a full-size delivery truck, help draw visitors through the different exhibit areas of the history gallery. A large-scale, three-dimensional diagram of ironmaking, steelmaking, and milling forms the backdrop of the steel gallery, and provides context for interactive exhibits.

Providing a multilayered multimedia experience

Video and audio exhibits provide a multi-sensory experience to communicate moods as well as messages. Archival audiovisual programming on an old-fashioned radio and television hint at a bygone era in the history gallery. Visitors are introduced to the steel gallery through an engaging show in the immersive Rhythm of Steel Theater.

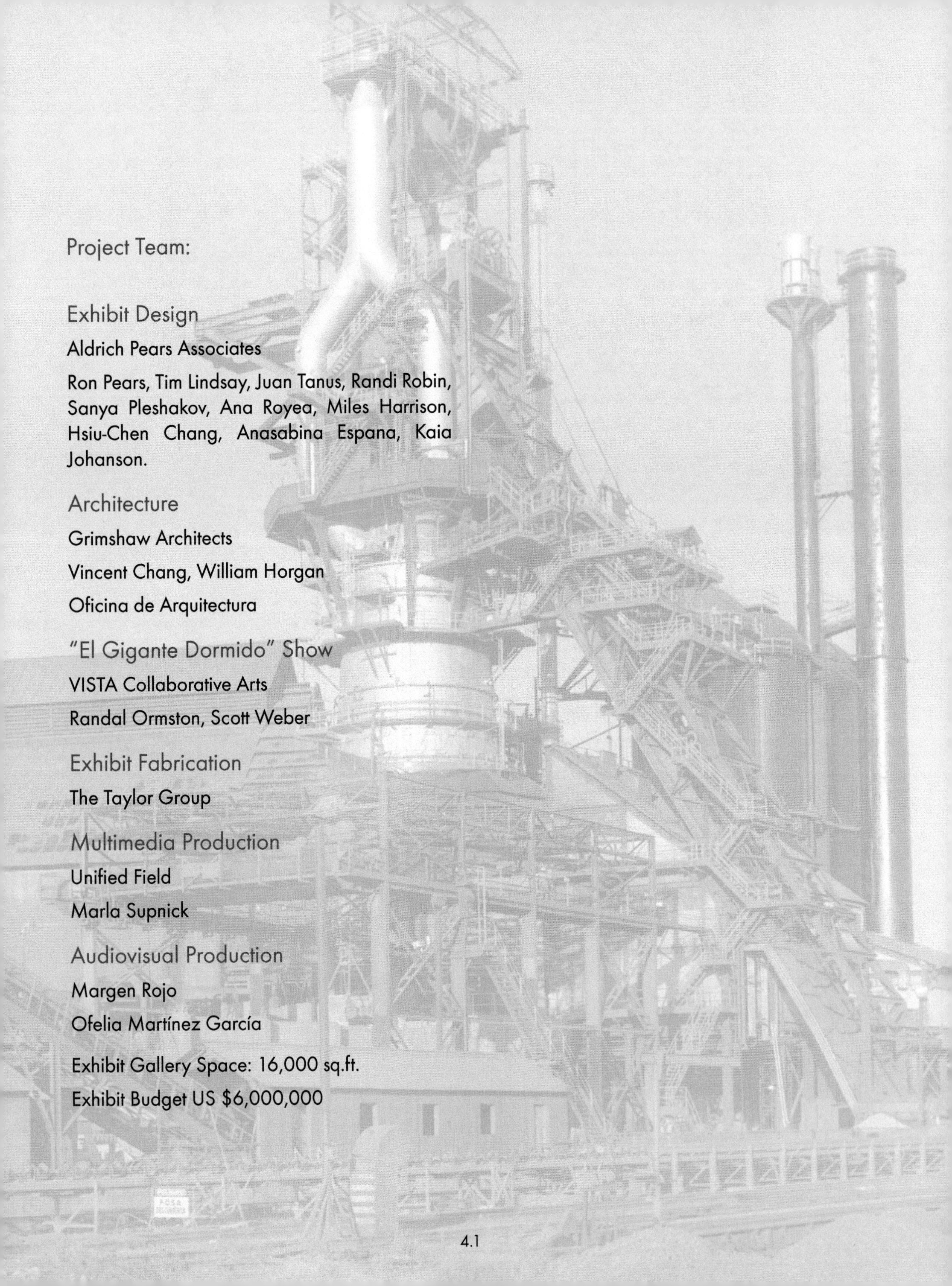

Project Team:

Exhibit Design

Aldrich Pears Associates

Ron Pears, Tim Lindsay, Juan Tanus, Randi Robin, Sanya Pleshakov, Ana Royea, Miles Harrison, Hsiu-Chen Chang, Anasabina Espana, Kaia Johanson.

Architecture

Grimshaw Architects

Vincent Chang, William Horgan

Oficina de Arquitectura

"El Gigante Dormido" Show

VISTA Collaborative Arts

Randal Ormston, Scott Weber

Exhibit Fabrication

The Taylor Group

Multimedia Production

Unified Field

Marla Supnick

Audiovisual Production

Margen Rojo

Ofelia Martínez García

Exhibit Gallery Space: 16,000 sq.ft.

Exhibit Budget US $6,000,000

Explore diferentes aspectos de este período a través
de un grupo de presentaciones multimedia - metraje de archivo, fotografías, audio
Explore different aspects of this period through clusters of multimedia exhibits -
archival footage, photographs, audio

Imágenes proyecta...
Projected images of audio...

Mural pintado que insinúa los problemas sociales y
económicos de la época
Painted mural that hints at the social and
economic troubles of this era

Panel con fotografías de eventos nacionales e internacionales
Panel with photographs of national and international events

Boletín de Noticias - Vea clips de noticias, entrevistas y
programación cultural de la época en un televisor a color
Newsflash - Watch news clips and interviews of the period on a color television

Museo del Acero involves a lot of firsts. It is the first time a blast furnace has been repurposed to function as a museum in Mexico, and it's the first time Mexico's story of steel has been told in an interpretive facility.

The museum's unique approach of combining history, science center exhibits, a special effects show, and a thrill ride will connect visitors to the steelmaking history of Mexico and inspire the country's future steel scientists and engineers ■

Credits: Sanya Pleshakov
AldrichPears Associates

MUSEUM OF THE HELLENIC WORLD:

Classical Metamorphosis

Museum of the Hellenic World in Athens, Greece focuses on the concept of a museum of narrative history. The design principle is based on the spatio-psychoanalytic concept of lack of artifacts (deeply routed in Greek culture) as a critique against the notion of 'collection' or 'acquisition'. The void or the emptiness is treated both as sense of loss of original artifacts as well as creative spatial process. This lack of collections led to the formulation of a new museological approach integrating exhibition and builiding into a metaphoric void of sorts.

4.2

Spatially, the building is conceived, as the mode of history, and highlighted both as the major diachronic documentation of Greek civilization and the main concept of the building: a spatial monument as opposed to a symbolic memorial. According to the Architect Nikos Georgiadis, light becomes one of the major design principles of the museum. "Light is not the means of seeing space, but it is part of the spatial process itself – a cultural principle" says Nikos. Light is an indigenous design principle common to all Mediterranean world. In his conversation with Picasso, the Greek poet Elytis once argued that the difference between surrealism in Greece and surrealism in Europe lies in the revelation of natural light.

The proposed continuous self-evolving strip structure across the building, produces homeo-morphic curved schemes in three distinct, spatial gestures/ installations:

- the amphitheatre introducing Classical Antiquity Lighting Treatment: Bright Daylight

- the dome introducing Byzantium Lighting Treatment: Indirect, Ambient, No-Shadows

- the sheltering cell introducing Modern times (17th - early 20th century), covering the overall museum space

Lighting Treatment: Cinematic Side-lighting, Long shadows

Yet, the strip surface employs a gradient synthesis of materials and construction techniques - varying from tectonic marble and stone, to cast material and finally timber, glass and metal. Financed by the Foundation of Hellenic World, the museum has a total exhibition space of 6000 sq.M.

The building is located in the Thematic Park of HELLENIC COSMOS on Piraeus Street in central Athens, Greece. The theme park includes the museum and other cultural and educational facilities designed by Anamorphosis Architects. Work on the park has commenced and the museum is scheduled to open in 2010.

Concept

The museum highlights three major historic periods in Greek civilization: Classical Antiquity, Byzantium and the Modern Times from the 17th to early 20th century involving the ultimate expatriation of the Greeks from Asia Minor in 1922, and the rise of new homelands in Greece. The museum will also emphasize the intermediate role of Prehistoric, Hellenistic, Roman and Ottoman periods. Anamorphosis proposed a spatial-psychoanalytic approach to Greek history which it regards as a permanent exchange between Greece and Asia Minor - the motherland and the "opposite side"- a region, both known and unknown.

The "missing" of the artifacts is seen as symbolic. The psychoanalytic concept of the lack of objects becomes the main design principle. Lack is the spatial critique of the narcissistic construction or de-construction of the object. It involves a familiarization with the loss of it the original, the beloved and a creative process of overcoming the loss, after a period of mourning. In this context the architects saw the void of objects as a real condition that recurs through Greek history. It also offered them an opportunity for developing a new, critical, narrative based approach to exhibition- a spatial museology – opposed to collections and acquisition.

Space, instead of becoming a neutral canvas for inscription of negativity and endless melancholic lament over the lost, is thereby activated through an exhibition that that draws on the subtle cues of the building material, lighting, progressive structural elements that evolve with elements of mixed-media installations destined to "replace" the absent artifacts. Anamorphosis designed a spatial monument, by reactivating the physicality of historic forms. The amphitheatre, the dome, and the self-sheltering structure, share a natural harmony with the landscape. These elements are real spatial experiences involving distinct qualities of lighting, material and collective function constantly recurring through Greek history. They are synthesized in

Southern night view, water installation

4.2

Modern Times installation, general view

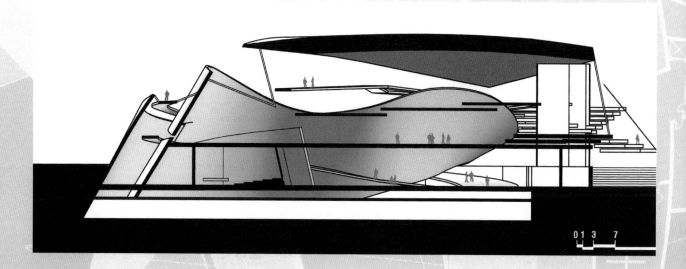

Plan: Section 1

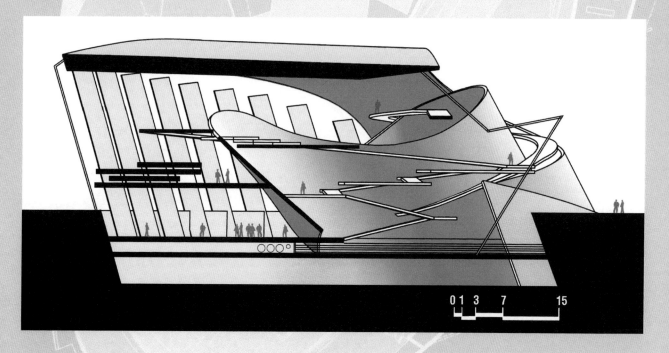

Plan: Section 2

one continuous gesture of morphic persistence and exchangeability across the three major spatial installations of the museum. The gallery space provides for three concentrations of people:

- Assembly or a meeting function in the amphitheatre
- Dense congregation in the dome
- A crowd exposed to a spectacular performance under the sheltering structure

The project of the THEMATIC PARK OF THE HELLENIC COSMOS involves the re-utilization and metamorphosis of a large dilapidated 60,000 sq.M. of industrial site and is the work of Architects Nikos Georgiadis, Tota Mamalaki, Kostas Kakoyiannis and Vaios Zitonoulis ■

Anamorphosis Architect Team

Plan 4: Byzantium, Ottoman period, 17th-18th centuries, 19th century

Project Brief
- **Exhibition Area: 6000 m^2**
- Preparation
  Landscapes
  Prehistory
  Antiquity
  Alexander The Great
  Hellenistic Period
  Byzantium
  Middle Ages / Ottoman Period
  Modern Times 17th-20th century
  New Homelands

- **Virtual Reality Cave: 374 m^2**
  Reception - exhibition space
  Waiting area
  Computer Control
  Computer room
  Cave

- **Visitor services: 1000 m^2**

- **Auxiliary Spaces: 1600 m^2**

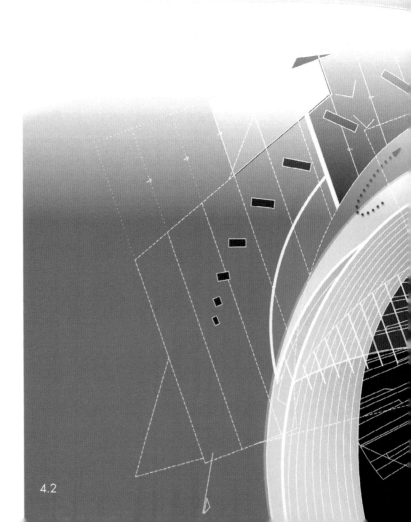

From left to right Lazaros Efraimoglou President of the Foundation of the Hellenic World [FHW], George Souflias, Minister of Public Works & Environment, and Dimitris Efraimoglou Managing Director of the Foundation of the Hellenic World.
Credit: FHW

From left to right Nikos Georgiadis (Anamorphosis Architects), Evangelos Venizelos Minister of Culture 2003, Kostas Kakoyiannis (Anamorphosis Architects), visitor, Panagiota Mamalaki (Anamorphosis Architects), at the 10th Anniversary of the Founding of the FHW.
Credits: Anamorphosis Architects.

GRAND EGYPTIAN MUSEUM:

The vast collections and architectural marvel that the Pyramids present are an incredible testimony to human spirit, imagination, perseverance and timeless quest to reach for the stars. With its collections crossing a staggering 160,000 large artifacts, the need to replace the existing 15,000 sq.M. facility established in 1902 has become a necessity. An ancient civilization built on the belief of bridging earth with heaven and the divinity of the Pharaohs posed more than one metaphoric challenge to the architects. They found an omniscient connector in LIGHT.

Architecturalizing the Face of Giza Plateau

4.3

LIGHT begat life and gave the Pharaohs the vision for creation 7000 years ago. The Grand Egyptian Museum was inspired by this vision to build an exceptional edifice to bring forth the grandeur of one of the greatest civilizations on earth.

Three significant design elements organise the Grand Egyptian Museum within the site:

- The Plateau Edge, which divides the site into higher and lower sections.
- The View towards the Pyramids.
- The Cairo-Alexandria Approach.

of the museum can be understood as a rhythm of structural (physical) and spatial (effective) folds within the Plateau face, architecturalizing and intensifying its timeless surface.

Space between Pyramids

The museum occupies a void within a 3-dimensional frame inscribed by a set of visual axes from the site to the three Pyramids. In plan, the lines that structure the museum are traced along these same visual lines. In section, the museum is structured along the ascent from the entrance and its parks to the Plateau level.

The Plateau

The proposal for the Grand Egyptian Museum begins by forming a new 'edge' to the Plateau, by creating a gentle slope as a thin veil of translucent stone structured by fractal geometry; opening and closing like folds within the desert sand. As seen from Cairo, this newly inscribed surface of translucent stone constructs a dynamic identity; yet from within the museum, this surface traces a new visual trajectory towards the Pyramids. The wall

Looking to Cairo

The new museum is located at the first desert plateau outside Cairo, between the Pyramids and Cairo. It acts at the intersection between Modernity and Antiquity, literally redirecting the traveller from the modernity of Cairo and Alexandria to the Ancient Heritage of the Egyptians. From an urban stand point, the museum is an 'inscription', inscribing the point at which the visitor changes direction from the city towards the Pyramids. The museum traces a new profile for the Plateau without competing with the Pyramids, utilising it's site and length to operate within the horizontal flows so indicative of modern vision and movement.

Fifth Façade

The New Museum is sited at the intersection of two cones of vision, the View to the Pyramids and the View to Cairo. The View to the Pyramids is inscribed into the spaces of the new Museum Complex, from its Open-Air System of parks to its precisely controlled environments of artefacts.

Two Bands of Light divide the site into three bands:

Lower Plateau: Infrastructural area to the road side

Ascent to Plateau: Cultural area of the GEM

Upper Plateau: Natural area of the Dunal Park.

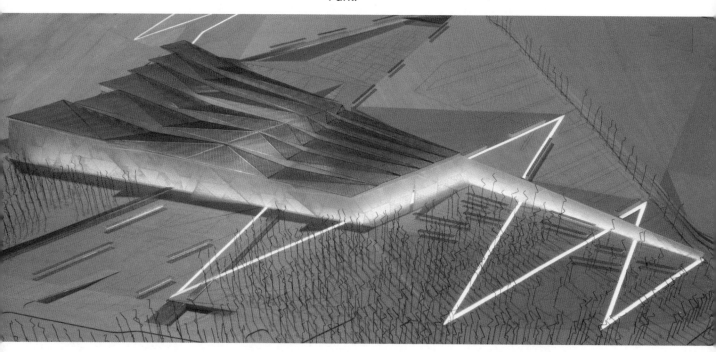

structural lines of the museum. The View to Cairo is traced by the path of the Nile Park which extends from the Dunal Park at the Plateau level, across the folds in the Roof and inscribed into the lines that define the Piazza as it extends to the city.

The structural folds that form the roof extend the dunal landscape of the site, maintaining the line of the desert plateau whilst constructing and spatialising a new horizon to view the city of Cairo.

Sculpting with Light

From the scale of the site to the scale of the display case, light carves and defines the Light excavates the primary systems of movement through the plateau, light-filled Grand Staircase, Void of the Translucent Stone Wall, Visual Causeway, Digital Streams.

Piazza/Sculpture Court

The Piazza is an space of gathering and exchange that begins the transition from the outside to the inside drawing visitors from the entrance forecourt to the lower level of the entrance lobby The Piazza is an active space both at night and during the day remaining active even when the museum/conference facilities are closed.

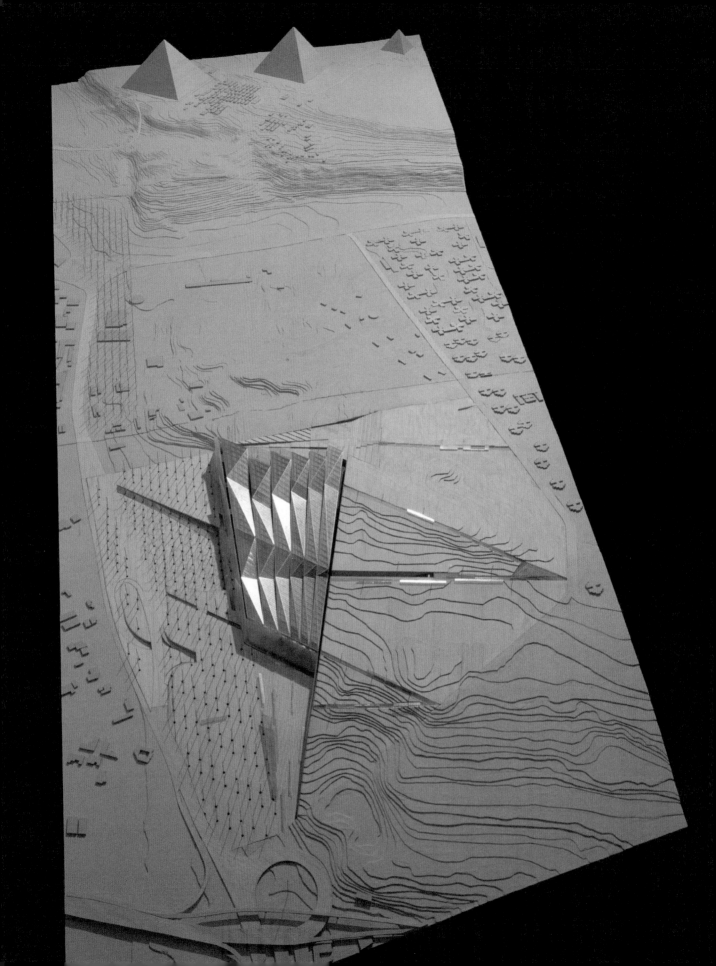

Lobby

Extending the transition from outdoor space to museum and conference, the lobby is an in-between space that is a continuation of the Piazza's exteriority into the planted shaded space of the lobby. The Nile Park flows through the lobby further integrating the exterior into the museum's interior.

Galleries

The permanent exhibition areas on the top floor are organised in five thematic bands within the structure constructed by the visual axes to the pyramids, the sixth band being the chronological route of the grand stair. Hypertextual nodes or Sculpture Garden Courts provide primary cross-movement between the

Grand Staircase

The Light-filled Grand Staircase ascends from the lobby to the permanent exhibition galleries on the top floor stopping off at special exhibitions, conservation workshops, temporary exhibition, and Archaeological Main Storage. The staircase is the chronological route within the museum, culminating in the view of the pyramids at the top of the stair. An identifiable reference point, the Grand Staircase allows visitors to easily navigate this vast collection.

thematic bands. The structural roof folds follow the spatial organisation of the thematic bands; controlled light is brought in through the roof folds. A clear organisation is provided to a large space yet still allowing flexible modes of display. The hyper-textural nodes form sculpture garden courts, which act as points of reference for the navigation of the collection also operate as rest-points for the visitor. One such point of reference is the court dedicated to Tutankhamun.

Tutankhamun Light Court is a triangular cut into the building that registers on the facade the importance of the collection inside. In certain areas the floor is excavated to allow the visitor to drop down into special rooms under the galleries where special exhibits occur.

Digital Streams

Paradoxically, the success of technological integration is its eventual disappearance-invisibility. In order to mesh technology into the new museum, technology is transformed into an architectural element; in this case into digital streams that operate spatially between the spatial bands that define thematic galleries. The walls that define the digital streams become the primary technology infrastructure element in the galleries supporting the interactive display requirements of individual vitrines.

The Grand Egyptian Museum is not a singular museum in the traditional sense of the museum, it is constructed as a complex of different activities which contribute to a cultural environment that is centred about Egyptology. By weaving different navigation routes through the complex, the world of ancient Egypt can be explored in different modes and levels. The museum is both a repository of cultural artefacts and an interactive cultural resource that celebrates the intersection of modernity with antiquity ■

Credits; Hennegen + Ping Architects
Reprint: Museum Design Fall 2007

4.3

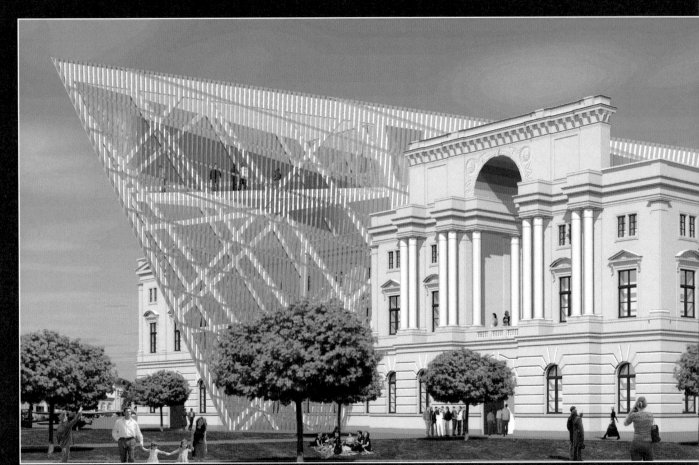

Cutting a Wedge

Central theme of the Military History Museum is the human being: those who went into the war and those who have remained at home; people of different eras and people of different generations. SDL is working with SIB Staatsbetrieb Saechsisches Immobilien und Baumanagement. The project is expected to be completed in 2009.

Daniel Libeskind designed the new extension by cutting a wedge through the structural order of the arsenal, giving the museum a place for reflection about organized violence. This wedge creats an objective view to the continuity of military conflicts and opens up vistas to central anthropological questioning.

The new extension gives a fundamental re-orientation to the existing building. It opens up the view to the historical center of Dresden. The wedge soars above the roof of the existing building, creating an image of modernization to the outside world and offering the opportunity to experience the opening to the city.

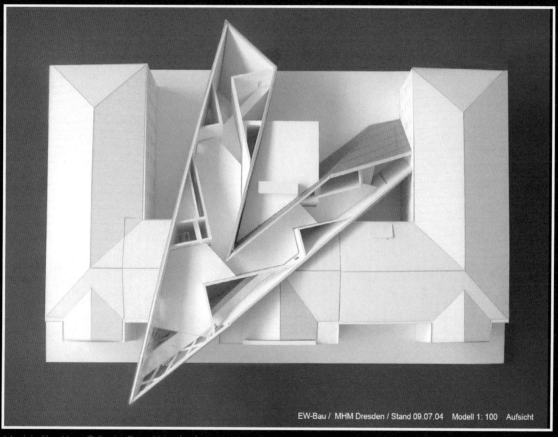

EW-Bau / MHM Dresden / Stand 09.07.04   Modell 1: 100   Aufsicht

Model , Plan View © Studio Daniel Libeskind

The new façade is being conceived against the background of the existing building, in response and contrast to it. The openness and transparency of the new façade stands against the opacity and solidity of the old façade. As one represents the severity of the authoritarian past in which it was built, the other reflects the openness of a democratic society and the changed role of its military. In the new elevation of the Museum both are visible at the same time and one through the other. This correlation corresponds to the juxtaposition of new and old in the building's interior; the rigid column grid of the old Arsenal is contrasted with a new column of free space. The interplay of both together forms the character of the new Military History Museum ▪

Reprint: Museum Design Fall 2008

Viewing Platform at Top of Wedge
Credit: Studio Daniel Libeskind

STONEHENGE VISITOR CENTER:

Extruded Earth

Completed around 1500 BC, the Stonehenge has an iconic presence shrouded in mystery, marvel and magic. Some speculate that it was a temple made for the worship while others attribute its purpose toward astronomical observations and associated rituals and burials. The construction of this mammoth configuration was an incredible engineering feat accomplished over 5000 years ago with embankment and ditch hoisting techniques using deer antlers and wood instruments. The chalk under the earth's surface was loosened and shoveled using cattle shoulder blades. The 80 bluestones of the inner circle that were moved from approximately 240 miles away, weigh up to 4 tons each, while the giant sarsen stones forming the outer circle, weighing as much as 50 tons each were moved 20 miles with a steeper terrain that may have required an estimated 600 men to move each one!

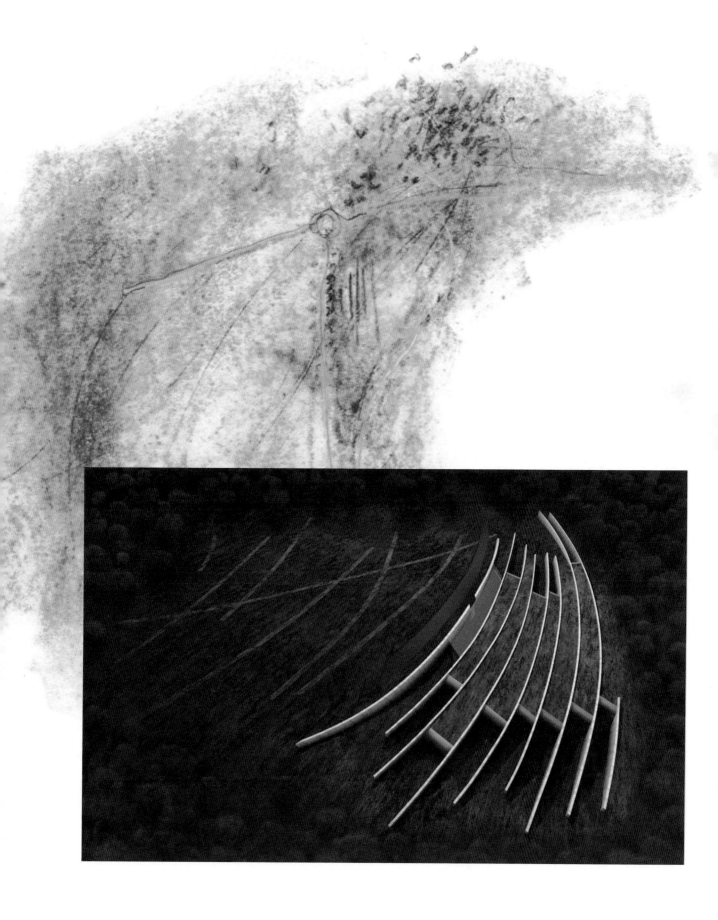

4.5

Situated in a vast plain in Wiltshire, surrounded by hundreds of round burial mounds, the Stonehenge site is a truly impressive awe-inspiring site. With a major highway running less than half-a mile away from the stones, the place is dotted with gift shops and hawkers selling everything from trinkets to food. The giant stones on the open down-land of Salisbury Plain two miles west of the town of Amesbury, Wiltshire, in southern England, are protected as a United Nations World Heritage Site with nearly 450 ancient monuments. The British government has a Master Plan to improve the setting of Stonehenge by reuniting it with its surrounding monuments and landscape. Removing the roads, fences and other commercial structures from around the stones will allow visitors to properly appreciate Stonehenge

and its landscape, as well as help with conservation efforts for the landscape and archaeology for future generations.

A visitor center project for this World Heritage site has been mired in controversy. A single level building, the visitor centre for English Heritage is conceived by the architects from Denton Corker Marshall as an abstract form embedded in and one with the surrounding landscape. Through exhibits and an integrated multi-media visitor experience, it will provide interpretation of the Stonehenge and the wider World Heritage Site.

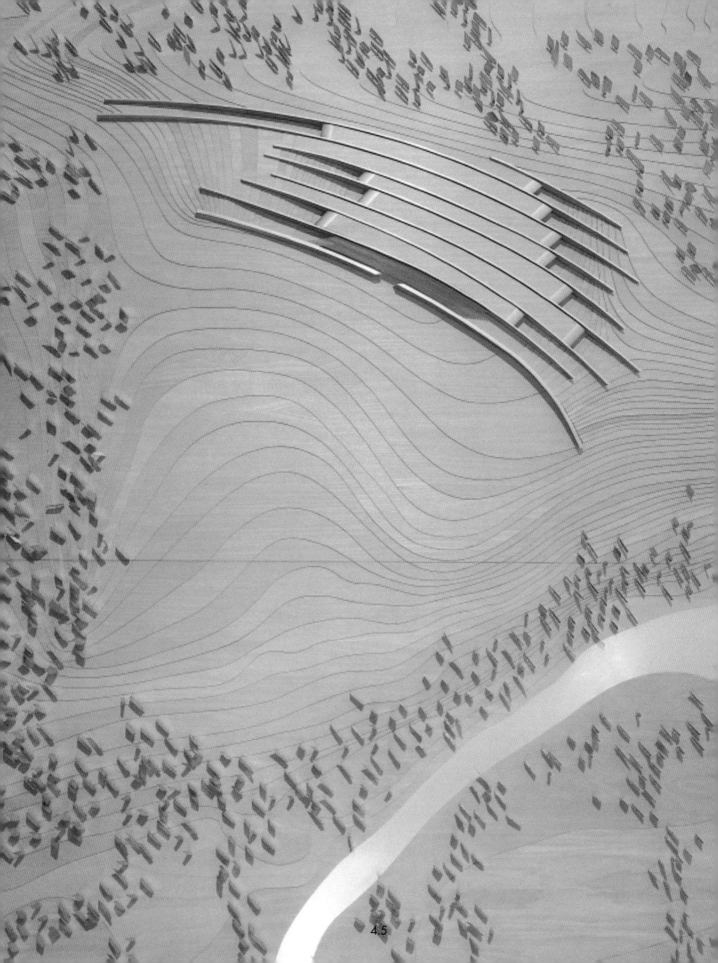

A series of planes slide and slice into the landscape to form the main part of the conceived building. These curved, apparently random abstract forms, read as powerful seams or layers extruded out of the earth. They carry with them the vaguest sense of geographical strata. They are metal clad, huge billets of pewter-toned burnished metal, establishing an image of solidity, strength and timelessness without recourse to stone, masonry or concrete, or any direct association with Stonehenge. They are of another language yet one sympathetic and respectful of the integrity of the monument and its ancient vocabulary.

There is no sense of the conventional building imagery; no apparent windows or architectural embellishments. The visual imagery gives little hint to the volumetric dimensions of the building and leaves much to inspired imagination. The wall becomes a pure landscape form, certainly powerful and impressive in its unambiguous clarity, but carrying none of the pretension of conventional architectural form-making.

This new Ł57m visitor center seeks to improve access to the World Heritage Site and returns it to the natural landscape devoid of highway traffic and the commercial opportunism that surrounds it presently ▪

Credits: Denton Corker Marshall

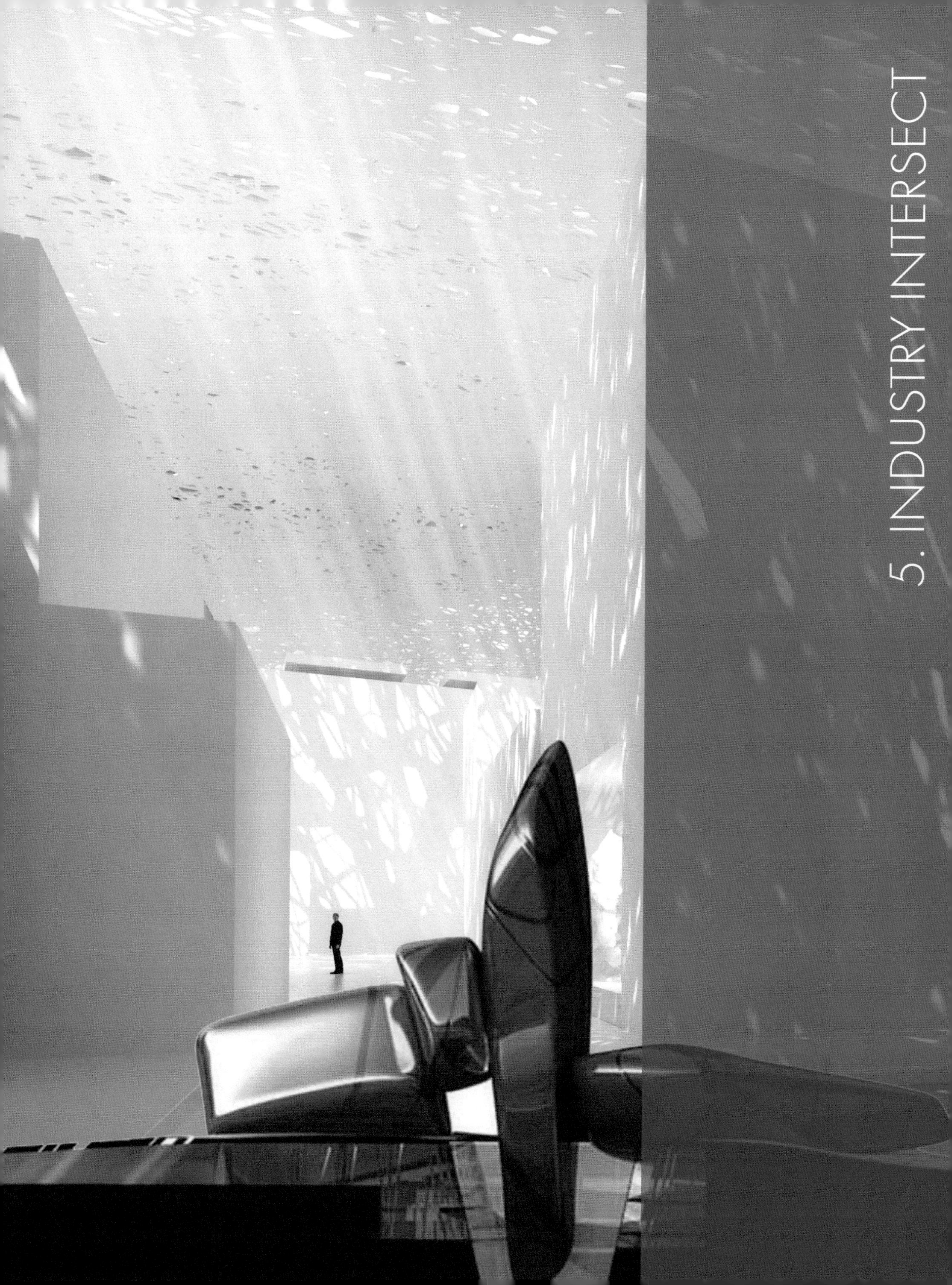

5. INDUSTRY INTERSECT

NEWSEUM:

Celebrating the First Amendment

The 250,000-square-foot museum of news offers visitors an experience that blends five centuries of news history with up-to-the-second technology and hands-on exhibits. TheNewseum is located between the White House and the U.S. Capitol and adjacent to the Smithsonian museums on the National Mall. The unique exterior architectural features include a 74-foot-high marble engraving of the First Amendment and an immense front wall of glass through which passers-by can watch the museum fulfilling its mission of providing a forum where the media and the public can gain a better understanding of each other.

The Newseum features seven levels of galleries, theaters, retail spaces and visitor services. It offers a unique environment that takes museum-goers behind the scenes to experience how and why news is made.14 main exhibition galleries explore news history, electronic news, photojournalism, world news and how the media covered major historical events.

The Newseum at night. Photo credit: Sam Kittner

Early United States Journals

1780

1810

To the press alone, ...ered as it is with abuses, the is indebted for all the triumphs which have been gained by reason and humanity over error and oppres...

News Corporation News History Gallery is built around the museum's collection of more than 30,000 historic newspapers — traces more than 500 years of news and includes five theaters that explore specific themes. The Cox Enterprises First Amendment Gallery includes artifacts and exhibits to dramatically establish the modern-day relevance of the five freedoms — religion, speech, press, assembly and petition — guaranteed by the First Amendment under the U.S. constitution.

Visitors in the **Time Warner World News Gallery** can watch television news and compare press freedoms in more than 190 countries. A major storyline of this gallery is the dangers reporters face around the globe while reporting the news. Dramatic icons — including a bullet-riddled, armor-reinforced pickup truck used by reporters and photographers in the Balkans — illustrate the dangerous conditions in which journalists often work.

Artist's rendering of News Corporation News History Gallery

Credits: Ralph Appelbaum Associates

Internet, TV, Radio.
Credits: Dorian Soto/Newseum

Internet, TV and Radio Gallery **is devoted to the history of electronic news, featuring a timeline tracing milestones in the growth of radio, television and Internet news; an exhibit on newsman Edward R. Murrow; a video on the emergence of cable TV and the development of Internet news in the digital age; and an original documentary that looks at the people and events from the "golden age" of television news (1947-1969).**

Gallery exhibits include Front Pages of 80 newspapers from around the world are updated daily with visitors having electronic access to more than 500 front pages. The adjacent terrace features an exhibit on the history of Pennsylvania Avenue and offers an unparalleled view of the U.S. Capitol building.

Pulitzer Prize Photographs Gallery **contains the largest and most comprehensive collection of Pulitzer Prize-winning photojournalism ever assembled. Visitors can**

Today's Front Pages. Artist's rendering courtesy Ralph Appelbaum Associates

view a Newseum documentary in which photographers explain their craft and can access an electronic database that will feature 1,000 images and 15 hours of video and audio compiled from interviews with 68 Pulitzer Prize-winning photographers.

9/11 Gallery is perhaps the first permanent museum exhibit devoted to the terrorist attacks of Sept. 11, 2001. This gallery looks at how the media — in New York and Pennsylvania, at the Pentagon and around the world — responded to one of the biggest news stories of the century, through Sept. 12 front pages, artifacts and a Newseum documentary that features journalists' accounts of their reactions that day.

Newseum also features one of the largest collections of original Berlin Wall sections outside of Germany with exhibits that examine the role of the media in the 30-year history of the wall.

The Journalists Memorial Gallery is a sweeping, two-story glass structure that will include more than 1,800 names of journalists who died while reporting the news from 1837 — Elijah Parish Lovejoy of The Alton (Ill.) Observer — through 2007. Each year, the Newseum will rededicate the memorial, adding the names of journalists who died on the job during the previous year. Other exhibits tell the compelling story of the urgency and universality of news through the ages. More than a dozen artifacts, including a clay brick with cuneiform writing (circa 1255-1235 B.C.) and a statue of Thoth, the Egyptian god of scribes (750 B.C.), reveal some of the many ways in which news traveled before the creation of the printing press in the 15th century.

ABC News Changing Exhibits Gallery explores a wide range of media issues with displays on breaking news, media trends,

Project Team

- Architect: Polshek Partnership Architects
- Exhibit Design: Ralph Appelbaum Associates
- Exhibit Production: Kubik Inc.
- Project Management: Tishman Speyer
- General Contractor: Turner Construction Co.

Artist's rendering of Cox Enterprises First Amendment Gallery.

Credits: Ralph Appelbaum Associates

news-event anniversaries and top photography. The gallery showcases original shows, traveling exhibits and displays developed in partnership with national and international media organizations and museums.

Pulliam Family Great Books Gallery features books and documents that help illustrate and illuminate the origins of freedom of the press. The oldest of the 20 works dates back more than 500 years to a 1475 printing of Thomas Aquinas' "Summa Theologica," a masterpiece that fused philosophy and theology. Other great

works on display include the Magna Carta, Thomas Paine's "Common Sense," and a 1787 first pamphlet printing of the U.S. Constitution. The documents are preserved in low light, but readable on interactive monitors through state-of-the-art page-turning software. The materials are on loan from the Remnant Trust.

NBC News Interactive Newsroom is a 7,000-square-foot interactive gallery, where visitors can select any of 48 interactive kiosks or experiences where they can immerse themselves in the many roles — photojournalist, editor, reporter, anchor — required to bring the news to the public. The gallery features eight "Be a TV Reporter" stations that allow visitors to choose from a variety of video backdrops, take their place in front of the screen, read their report from a TelePrompter and see themselves in action. A unique "group interactive experience" called the Ethics Table challenges two teams

Artist's rendering of Walter and Leonore Annenberg Theater
Credits: Cortina Productions

of players to correctly answer a series of ethical questions and be the first to fill in the front page of their team's newspaper.

The Newseum is one of the most technologically advanced museums in the world. The Newseum ordered 100 miles of fiber-optic cable to link up-to-the-second technologies that include electronic signage and interactive kiosks, two broadcast studios, 15 theaters and a 40 x 22-foot high-resolution media screen. The Newseum also features a food court, two-level Newseum Store and a special entrance on the C Street side of the building for groups. In addition to the Newseum, the building includes a two-level, 24,000-sq ft. conference center, a three-level restaurant — "The Source by Wolfgang Puck" — and more than 140,000 sq ft. of residential apartments. The 643,000 sq.ft. complex has cost nearly $450 million including $100 million in property costs ■

Credits: Newseum
Reprint: Museum Design Spring 2008

HARLEY-DAVIDSON MUSEUM:

An American ICON

In March 2005, the City of Milwaukee and the Harley-Davidson Motor Company signed formal agreements for the purchase of the 20 acre parcel of land at the corner of Sixth and Canal Streets near downtown Milwaukee in Wisconsin. Rapidly unveiling the design for the museum, Harley-Davidson broke ground at the museum site on June 1, 2006.

Nearly two years in the making the 130,000 sq.ft facility is spread across three buildings that will house the Harley-Davidson Museum and Archives, restaurant, café, retail and special events zone.

The museum celebrates an American Icon- a Legend in its own right. It is a place where riders and non-riders alike come together to experience freedom, camaraderie and pride that Harley-Davidson riders feel every time they fire up their motorcycles. The museum envisions a global community of people coming together to take part in the rich history of the Company, the passion of the

View of Harley-Davidson Museum from the corner of Canal & Sixth Street

riders, the stories of the employees, dealers, suppliers, company leaders and community members. With projected attendance figures in the 350,000 range annually, the museum is expected to generate significant tax revenue and regional economic growth for the Milwaukee communities through over $78 million in annual spending.

The exhibits showcase legendary motor-cycles including the famous Serial Number ONE – the first ever-built in 1903. Other exhibits include Elvis Presley's 1956 Harley-Davidson KH motorcycle and the 13 feet long "King Kong" that was customized over a 40 year period, among others. Visitors are able to explore the personalized Living the Legends rivets that contain stories, experiences and connections that many have with this legendary American icon. Thousands of rivets are displayed on steel walls and the plaza of the museum complex.

Elvis Presley's 1956 Harley-Davidson KH motorcycle

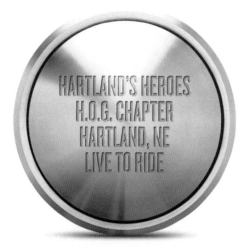

Living the Legends Rivets

Harley-Davidson Museum's Living the Legends area

Beyond the inspiring exhibits, the museum grounds feature, open green spaces where riders and visitors can socialize and enjoy the Milwaukee riverfront. The building architecture draws its inspiration from striking industrial and urban design elements such as exposed glass and steel to reflect the industrial history of Harley-Davidson and Milwaukee. The roads within the site restore the historical city grid and serve as cross-roads of the Harley-Davidson neighborhood. A river-walk bordering the perimeter of the grounds on three sides allows visitors to enjoy its park-like settings.

The museum ultimately tells authentic stories of riders who have made their dreams come true ∎

Harley-Davidson through History...

The 2008 Harley-Davidson XL 1200N SPORTSTER

Credits: The Harley Davidson Museum

Reprint: Museum Design Spring 2008

MERCEDES-BENZ MUSEUM:

Endorsing Excellence

Mercedes-Benz Museum intricately combines structure, style and content. The Museum is dedicated to the world's most legendary car and it's synonimous brand identity. Its unique structure has been specifically devised to showcase a collection in which technology, adventure, attractiveness and distinction are merged. It is also a Museum for people to freely move through, to dream, learn, look and let themselves be oriented by fascinations, light and space...

It is a Museum for the city, a new landmark to celebrate the enduring passion of Stuttgart's most famous inventor and manufacturer.

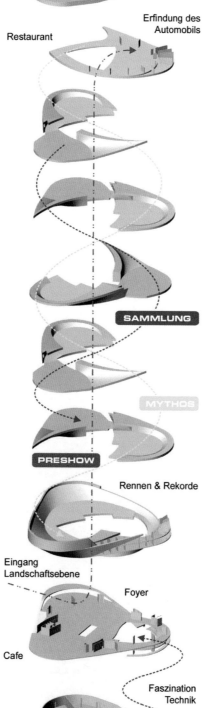

Erfindung des
Automobils

Restaurant

SAMMLUNG

MYTHOS

PRESHOW

Rennen & Rekorde

Eingang
Landschaftsebene

Foyer

Cafe

Faszination
Technik

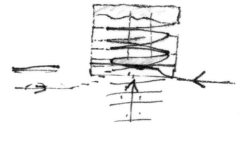

5.3

The structure of the Mercedes-Benz Museum is based on a trefoil. Both in its internal organization and in its outward expression this geometry responds to the car-driven context of the museum. Inside, walking down the ramps of the Museum, surrounded by cars of different ages and types, the visitor is reminded of driving down the highway. Outside, the smooth curves of the building echo the rounded vernacular of nearby industrial and event spaces, such as the soccer stadium, the Mercedes-Benz test course, and the gas and oil tanks along the river, as well as the recurrent loops of the road system on site.

The building also implicitly radiates the qualities that we see as the best of our times; good quality materials, durability, character, neatness. In its materialization the Mercedes-Benz Museum reproduces the values that we associate with Mercedes-Benz: technological advancement, intelligence, and stylishness. Once inside, visitors feel both stimulated and comfortable.

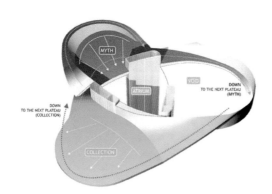

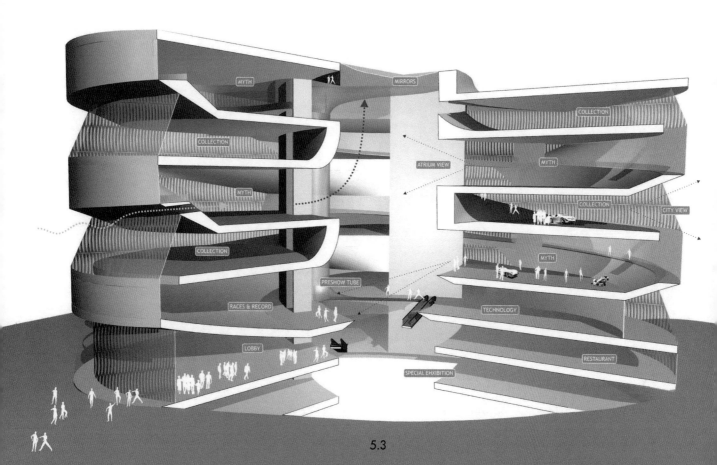

The 25,000 m² Mercedes-Benz Museum is situated next to the Daimler-Chrysler Untertuerkheim plant on a raised platform which also offers room to the Vehicle Center. Visitors enter the building from the northwest corner. The entrance lobby introduces to the visitor the organizational system of the Museum, which entails the distribution of the two types of exhibitions over three

'leaves', which are connected to a central 'stem' in the form of an atrium. The entrance lobby, besides practical functions, contains an escalator that leads down to the ground level, and three lifts that take visitors up to the top of the building.

The visitor proceeds through the Museum from top to bottom; during the ride up the atrium, visitors are provided with a multimedia Preshow presentation. The two aspects of the museological arrangement, the collection of cars and trucks and the Myths, are ordered chronologically from top to bottom, starting with the three oldest cars at the top floor in the display dedicated to the invention of the car. From this starting point at the top, the +eight level, the visitor may take one of two spiralling ramps down; the first chain linking the collection of cars and trucks, and the second the connecting Mythos rooms, which are the secondary displays related to the history of Mercedes Benz. The two spiralling trajectories cross each other continuously, mimicking the interweaving strands of a DNA helix, thus making it possible for the visitor to change trajectories.

The downward incline of the two interlocking trajectories is confined to the ramps at the perimeter of the building only; the platforms that function as display areas themselves are level, with the slow gradients of the walkways bridging the height differences between them. The platforms, the 'leaves' of the trefoil, are arranged around the central 'stem' of the atrium in This structure generates exciting spatial constellations, enabling a wide range of look-through options, shortcuts, enclosed and open spaces, and the potential for continuity and cross-references in the various displays.

The collection of cars and trucks is shown in combination on five plateaus. Seven plateaus show the Myths and, at the lowest levels, Races and Records and the Fascination of Technology. At ground level, below the elevated landscape, and accessed by the escalator at the entrance level, are the Children's Museum, several small shops and a restaurant, housed in a large and open-plan space that connects the Museum to the nearby Vehicle Center ■

PHASE I

Dach
E8
E7

Rohbau im Bau / fertiggestellt

E6

Glasfassade im Bau / fertiggestellt

E5
E4

Technik / Ausbau

E3
E2

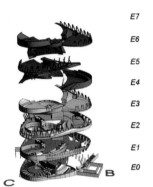

E1
E0

C   B

PHASE II

Dach
E8
E7

Rohbau im Bau / fertiggestellt

E6

Glasfassade im Bau / fertiggestellt

E5
E4

Technik / Ausbau

E3
E2
E1

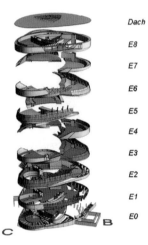

E0

C   B

PHASE III

Dach
E8
E7

Rohbau im Bau / fertiggestellt

E6

Glasfassade im Bau / fertiggestellt

E5
E4

Technik / Ausbau

E3
E2
E1

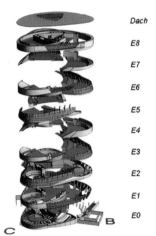

E0

C   B

PHASE IV

Dach
E8
E7

Rohbau im Bau / fertiggestellt

E6

Glasfassade im Bau / fertiggestellt

E5
E4

Technik / Ausbau

E3
E2

Musealer Ausbau

E1
E0

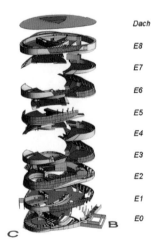

C   B

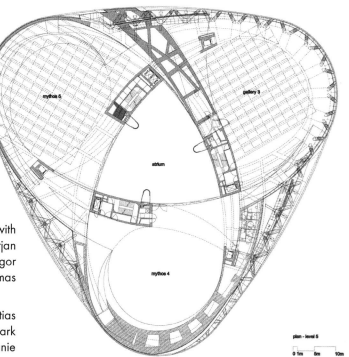

plan - level 5

0 1m   5m   10m

Project Team

UN Studio: Ben van Berkel, Tobias Wallisser, Caroline Bos with Marco Hemmerling, Hannes Pfau, Wouter de Jonge, Arjan Dingsté, Götz Peter Feldmann, Erwin Horstmanshof, Gregor Kahlau, Björn Rimner ,Alexander Jung, Mike Herud, Thomas Klein, Simon Streit, Taehoon Oh

In collaboration with: Wenzel + Wenzel, Karlsruhe: Matias Wenzel, Markus Schwarz, Clemens Schulte-Mattler, Mark Schwesinger, Ina Karbon, Christoph Friedrich, Stefanie Hertweck

Structure and Facade: Werner Sobek Ingenieure, Stuttgart

Geometry advisor: Arnold Walz

Climate engineering: Transsolar Energietechnik, Stuttgart

Cost estimator: Nanna Fütterer

Infrastructure: David Johnston, London

KING ABDUL AZIZ CENTER
FOR KNOWLEDGE & CULTURE

In competition with some of the world's greatest architects, Snohetta won the competition for designing Saudi Arabia's new Cultural Center for the world's largest oil company- Saudi Aramco, celebrating its 75th anniversary. On May 20, 2008, King Abdullah bin Abdulaziz set the cornerstone for the Cultural Center which will house a museum, library, theater, cinema and more. The building reflects the history of oil in Saudi Arabia and is different from the country's architectonic traditions with its abstract and spectacular form.

Located on Dammam Dome, the iconic structure will stand alongside the site of Prosperity Well No.7, the first well in Saudi Arabia to yield oil in commercial quantities.

The founder of the modern state of Saudi Arabia, King Abdulaziz envisioned a forward-thinking, advanced Kingdom propelled by Saudi energy and determination. The Center, which will contribute to the future of the Kingdom and the humanity by promoting knowledge, cross-cultural understanding and an appreciation of diversity, will

honor his vision for his country and his commitment to modernization.

According to Aramco Oil Company CEO Abdallah S. Jum'ah, it will serve the community's needs in the fields of knowledge, culture and the arts and be a source of enrichment that will inspire younger generations to reflect on the golden era of Islamic culture. The Center will open to public in 2012. Designed with a cafe-like atmosphere, the Center's library will combine digital access to information, connectivity with knowledge centers across the world and an extensive array of books and periodicals.

The Center's museum will showcase the rich history and legacy of the Kingdom of Saudi Arabia. Its programs and exhibits will connect the past with the future and fire the imagination of visitors of all ages. An exhibition hall will be the focal point for bringing cultures of the world to Saudi Arabia through exhibitions that stimulate cross-cultural engagement and appreciation. A Children's Education Center will offer an innovative and creative museum and library designed specifically for children from 2-12 years old. The purpose of

vibrant cultural life of the center to the past and to the very roots of the society from which this center is conceived.

The architectural concept is based upon the following six principles:

The Past and the Future

Culture grows out of the past, without culture no community or company can create a future. The design for the Saudi Aramco Cultural Center embraces both past and future, captured in the

this facility is to spark in children a love of learning. Children will discover captivating objects and immersive multimedia exhibits that will incorporate storytelling, and self-directed study to encourage interaction and true hands-on learning.

Located in Dhahran in the Eastern Province the King Abdulaziz Cultural Center will provide for a wide range of activities serving the local population and becoming a cultural landmark on both a regional, national and global horizon. When completed, the project will contain some 45 000m2 of facilities. The museum and archive facilities connect the

present. Both in terms of architectural expression and internal logic this proposal digs down into the past and reaches up in to the future.

Introvert and Extrovert

The King Abdulaziz Center for Knowledge and Culture concept is both introverted and extroverted. Below grade the museum and archive functions are grouped around the inner void looking inwards to the truths and knowledge to be found within Saudi Aramco and the Kingdom of Saudi Arabia. Above grade, the composition reaches out of the ground, connecting to the world beyond.

Repository and Beacon

Located below grade the Museum and Archive becomes a true repository of knowledge, in protective surroundings and stored for posterity. In contrast the Library, Children's Exhibit and Visitor Centre are expressed as beacons to scholars across the world.

Diversity and Unity

This design takes the form of a complex composition, consisting of a number of individual and discrete components. Balance and harmony is created

Energy

The balance and harmony of the King Abdulaziz Center for Knowledge and Culture composition is not static, but dynamic, expressive of the team work and above all of the energy to be found in the people that comprise Saudi Aramco and Saudi Arabia. Evoking wonder and bearing memory of the steadfast endurance and hard labour under severe conditions in the pioneer striking of oil ■

through interdependence. Each component is fashioned as a unique and tailor- made entity, conforming to and expressive of its own individual needs and requirements.

Teamwork

No one component can be removed. All are interdependent and rely upon each other. The resulting composition is an expression of team work. Each part can be endlessly adjusted to suit the individual and specific needs. This form for flexibility is not general or universal, but specific and individual.

Credits: Snohetta Architects

CHENGDU CENTER FOR THE ARTS:

Floating-Stone Urbanism

Designed by the Rotterdam based MVRDV Architects, the Chengdu Center for the Arts offers an interesting mix of functional iterations in a dazzling visual vocabulary.

The questions that the planners and architects explored while creating the masterplan for the center grappled with some of the primary needs of the premise including how a facility of this magnitude sustain itself and contribute to the living culture and regional development of the communities it seeks to serve.

Brother and Sister

The Chengdu Center for the Arts complex
will incorporate a music hall, cinema theater,
a conference center and the new museum
for contemporary art. The complimentary
relationship between the various functional
elements of the building gives it a culturally
symbiotic brother-sister relationship. The over-
arching Yin-Yang balance is achieved through
the use of form and materials. For example, the

glass façade of the main building is contrasted
with the solid surface treatment, while the
symmetrical elements are juxtaposed with the
a-symmetrical.

Halls

The grouping of museum programs with the
theater and conference space generates a
Great Hall for the Arts. Various theaters in this
hall appear like solid stones or jewels. The

theaters are carefully positioned in relation to the Opera Hall located next to the main road across the Ocean World to allow visitors to spill out towards the main front of the building. The Concert Hall faces the river allowing for a beautiful backdrop of the concerts to connect with the surrounding neighborhoods. The backstage can be opened up to the nature to allow for an added environment to the stage set through unique urban windows.

Arcades

By pushing the lowest floor of the Hall upwards, it gives way to passages to the heart of the building. The paths open the complex so that it connects different parts of the Ring Park . The resulting arcades are populated with terraces, kiosks, information booths, ticket counters, restaurants and bars. These large open spaces can also offer events, performances,

open concerts and outdoor art shows and installations. The morphology is acoustically conducive for audio performances.

Museum

The undulating floor that forms the base of the museum hall is a new topography that allows for a unique configuration. Every location offers a different quality of exhibit environment within the museum. There are terraces with an overview of the displayed art inside or out, valleys and pockets offer shelter for more intimate viewing spaces, among many other improvisations and grotto-like alcoves. Specificity is combined with flexibility expanding the Ring Park with public art blended into the landscape.

Hill

The roof of the museum is draped over the solid stones "sewn" into the carpet. For this reason the roof undulates just as the lower level does. The roof experience is like that of a sequence of valleys and hill tops- an inhabitable landscape that can act as outdoor sculpture gardens and theater pockets. The valleys are acoustically sheltered from the roar and noise of the nearby highway traffic. By slanting the garden to ground level at opposite ends, a public terrace of sorts is created that turns the main building into a public hill of sorts, extending and elevating the public park. The hill offers breathtaking panoramic views of the surroundings.

The Ring Park can be seen as a chain of pearls of green spaces with a series of water gardens. Papyrus and waterlily filled basins connect the park with the riverand create an ecological leisure land attracting dragonflies and birds. The pool water could be used for partial cooling of the building and serves as a filter for grey water draining off the roof.The waterways and the

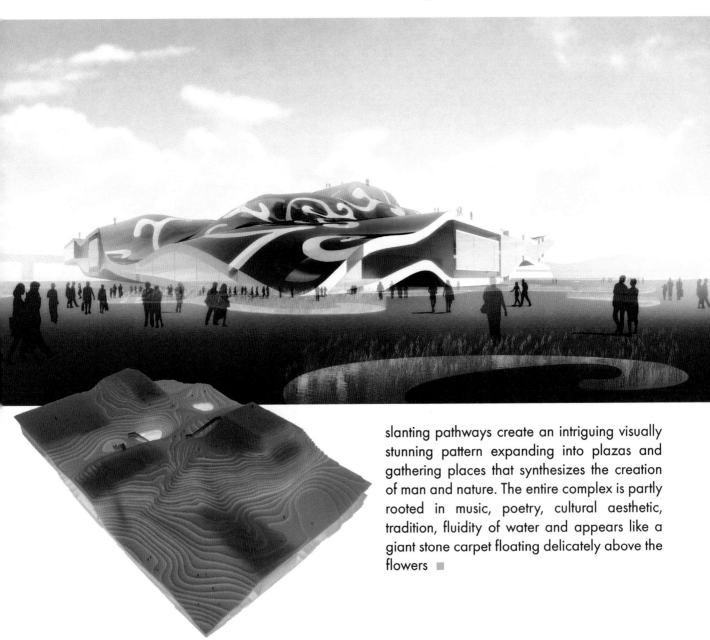

slanting pathways create an intriguing visually stunning pattern expanding into plazas and gathering places that synthesizes the creation of man and nature. The entire complex is partly rooted in music, poetry, cultural aesthetic, tradition, fluidity of water and appears like a giant stone carpet floating delicately above the flowers ■

Credits: MVRDV Architects

Project Brief

Client: Chengdu Exhibition & Travel Group
Program: Theater and Art Museum
Total Covered Space: 80,000 sq.M.
Competition: 2007

Project Team

Architects: Winy Maas, Jacob van Rijs, Nathalie deVries
Structure: Arup Beijing Rory McGowan
Acoustics: Artec NY, Tataeo Nakajima
Model: MBM Delft
Renders: Oceanpic Beijing

Future Forward is about possibilities. Museums are evolving and transforming themselves and the lives of their diverse audiences. They are seeking new definitions, new approaches, new meanings and new opportunities to enhance learning and bring about sustainable change. The spectrum of projects, industry intersect, living culture and mixed use studio concepts featured in this book offer a glimpse into the shape of things to come in the decades ahead, as museums continue to grow in myriad ways adapting to the changing needs of experiential learning and collective memory.

Credits: Zaha Hadid Architects   Cairo Expo City

What was traditionally within the domain of curatorial academe is increasingly being influenced by those considered "outside" the arteries of museology per se. Exhibits themselves are on the cusp of moving into the fifth generation- from the days of the early museums and science centers- from collections based presentations, story-based or themed to interactive hands-on and didactic, immersive scenic and multi-media infused learning environments to those exhibits that offer a visitor-driven presentation of projected outcomes and scenario-building experiences.

There is even a Museum of Tomorrow (MOT) in Taipei conceived by JUT Foundation, Chungtai Changhung Construction Company, and Ppaper, open 24 hours a day telling the visitors: "A better tomorrow awaits your visit" as it strives to connect creativity, culture, environment, innovation and aesthetics in different ways. MOT is designed to be nomadic and shift its location frequently. A different approach to learning spawned by the internet is

Credits: Zaha Hadid Architects

450,000 sqm² sculpted city for exhibitions and conferences.

inevitable both at individual and social levels that would impact museums as institutions of non-formal experiential learning, hubs of cultural gathering places and nodes of revival. Chatrooms, blogs, twitters and the facebooks of our times will soon see unpredictable transformational growth.

According to Tom Hennes, Principal of the New York based Thinc Design, the widespread public access to information and, even more importantly, the radical ease with which communities can surf through the Internet, open broad new opportunities for musems to be designed as flexible resources that can be accessed and utilized in many different ways by many different groups and individuals. This suggests a profound transition in the way museums interpret their collections and in the stories they tell, from a fixed narrative (the museum as preserver of culture or nature) to a dynamic system of narratives (the museum as a contact zone among communities, and a place of ongoing

Water Planet Exhibit at the California Academy of Sciences, showing one of the island interactive surfaces in use. Showing adaptations to gradients of salinity, with an 'imager' spurts water from its peaked vents.

Credits: Tom Hennes, Thinc Design

California Academy of Sciences

knowledge creation). It means that the design of museum must increasingly blend the core attributes of museums as places that hold authentic collections and the potential for exhibits to immerse their users in a particular experience, with the attributes of dynamic information systems to enable museums to generate evolving meanings and interpretation through a continuum of dialogue between their creators and their users.

Museum architecture is increasingly embracing a visual symbolism that is both timeless and futuristic in more ways than one. Globalization is beginning to affect cross-cultural dialog at various levels and their impact on the future of museums is yet to be fully discerned. The catalytic coordination of professional resources and implementation dynamics is expanding possibilities of reach and outreach resulting in remarkable optimization of financial and intellectual resources.

Museum designers from different continents are cross-pollinating their creative rigors on to the creation of national museums obtuse to their own cultural backgrounds. Not only has the last

Painted matte silver, the walls reflect light and projection with a precisely controlled luminosity. A seamless surround video is projected onto the walls every hour.

Credits: Tom Hennes, Thinc Design

California Academy of Sciences

decade seen an increased blurring of geo-political boundaries and national identities, it has experienced an unprecedented fluidity of resources that has re-shaped the manifestation of culture and heritage. From conventional leanings of curatorial practices to the frayed edges of neo-economic colonialism, museums face a plethora of challenges as they seek relevance while engaging diverse audiences.

Understanding the immediate needs of institutional planning, while addressing the larger human needs to learn from our shared and unshared histories, our many pasts, our present and our collective future, will increasingly shape the mission of museums in times to come. Resonance with the pulse of pluralistic societies in dynamic flux, will guide the process of exercising judgment, while advancing the continuum of museums as centers of education, equity and excellence.

Visual Vocabulary

Inter-cultural dialogue is changing the way architects and

Credits: G. Jacob

Saadiyat Island Cultural District, Abu Dhabi

designers are approaching the visual manifestation of new museum projects creating a new level of broader subtlety in aesthetic appreciation. Examples abound in cross-cultural interface where one can observe a Japanese architects designing museums in Saudi Arabia or Irish architects transforming a museum project in Egypt or Dutch architects tackling urbanism with a cultural tilt in Korea. The architects and designers themselves are often displaced and nomadic in their spheres of education, training, travels, business locations, cultural sensitivity and interests. As their visual vocabulary expands, so does their palette of creative thought and innovative cross-fertilization. Their ability to rise above a traditional mindset and inspire generations, is often lauded by museum trustees and boards who are increasingly appreciative of fresh-thinking, sensitivity and its potential impact on regional development. Design for design's sake, can only carry the vision so far. Ultimately, the litmus test is in the resonance of the selected visual vocabulary with the

Credits: G. Jacob

450,000sq.ft. Guggenheim Abu Dhabi Museum designed by Architect Frank Gehry, Saadiyat Island

institutional mandate of the museum based on the experiential content. The iconic buildings are 3D extensions of institutional brands seeking marketability and sustained credibility.

Globalization

While methodology of museum planning, process, procurement, production and project management are getting increasingly standardized, globalization is also triggering resource-pooling and out-sourcing of various services traditionally held to socio-geographic confines of a region. Design drawings, templates, construction materials, applications and expertise are streaming through a realm of fast pace transportation, internet and skype-laden design-build briefings and presentations. New software programs like Generative Components ™, CATIA ™ and many others are beginning to enable architects and engineers to generate free-form sustainable buildings, green materials and methods of integration. Programs and customized models offer options and alternate solutions reducing remodeling and

THE MIT MEDIA LABORATORY
City Car

A lightweight, intelligent, electric vehicle that radically reduces urban energy consumption and carbon footprints.

Credits: KPC Design

MIT Museum

redesign time significantly. Cutting-edge tools like Selective Laser Sintering (SLS) allows for fusing together layers of nylon powder into a 3D model by a computer-directed heat laser creating scintillating building models that enable rapid prototyping. The seamless integration of communication between museum clients, architects, designers, curators, museum educators, fund-raisers, board-members, trustees and potential donors, is already generating a transformational impact in the ways museums are being conceived, funded and built.

Even as the planning and design-build process transcends geo-political boundaries, crosses over time-zones and melts language barriers, globalization faces a bit of a conundrum associated with the sense of place. Traditional forms, motifs and indigenous techniques ensure cultural continuity and reinforce a sense of identity, while architectural experimentation promotes innovation, adaptability and osmosis associated with iterations of 'international style'. Architectural franchising is also on the rise

Ed Krent, Principal Krent/Paffet/Carney Inc.
Credits: KPC Design

MIT Museum

where iconic national and cultural symbols are often dictated by the styles of lead architects and design principals. Walking into a museum in the United States could as well be linked with the experiential visit to a museum in, say, Germany- planned by the same master-planners, architects, designers and interpretive teams- all part of a subtle class of conforming to a standardized experimentation with space and methods of communication.

Synergistic Materials

Museum architecture of the new millennium is revisiting the conventional palette of construction material into a vocabulary that speaks to the exhibits in more ways than one. With material

Credits: MVRDV Architects.   Gwanggyo Power Center

applications across conventional lines increasing exponentially like social networking groups through Venn-like intersects, bio-mimicry, bio-degradability and bio-energy are on the overdrive as never before. The building materials are beginning to promote values that answer their co-relationship with their environments. An intelligent adaptation of sustainable and smart materials is steadily making in-roads into a design dialog within the parenthesis of the emotive and the rational. Cross pollination of ideas from materials and technology firms to hi-tech research labs, automotive industry, defense and innovative applications developed by NASA (National Aeronautics and Space Administration) and other research institutions around the world, have yielded a plethora of possibilities for museum designers and architects with museum buildings open to increasing levels of experimentation.

Neo-Urbanism

Younger cities and those in the throes new development are seeing a more rapid revival than the established meccas of

Credits: MVRDV Architects

Gwanggyo Power Center

culture. The hunger and desire to experiment and make a statement is more pronounced in those domains than elsewhere, where a new breed of approaching and embedding museums is being spawned by the futurists.

The Gwanggyo Power Centre designed by MVRDV Architects near Seoul, Korea is a futuristic 6.5 million sq.ft. neo-urban project that weaves in museums, leisure, education, office, retail, housing and other facilities into a continuum of dwelling, sustainable growth. The design is intended to mimic and offer a seamless link between constructed and natural environmental space. It was conceived in rings because the town has different needs for phasing, positioning, and size. Every structure has a terrace with plantations for outdoor life. The plantations are fed by a floor-to-floor circulation system that stores water for irrigation. The end result is a vertical park that reduces energy and water usage. Imagine a museum and science center 'destination' embedded in this environment with exhibits

714,400 sq.ft. Kring-KumHo Culture Complex in Seoul, Korea designed by UnSangDong Architects.

that explain the mechanics of the functioning of the gigantic complex, materials used and advantages to an inherent set of sustainable lifestyle choices.

Imagine, then, the breathtaking sense of possibility involved in the creation of an entirely new city whose primary purpose is to impact its residents in more than one ways. The challenge of

Gale International's Songdo City in Korea is to create a city that inspires more than the footprint of the enabling technology and amenities that it provides for value-creation. Currently under construction, this incredible complex includes a 100 acre central park, schools, hospitals, hotels, retail, 30 million sq.ft. of residential space, an Ecotarium, Museum and 10 million sq.ft. of green space , among others, offering an unparalleled new level of excellence in living, learning and working, while remaining connected globally with the highest penetration of broadband technologies on earth creating a "ubiquitous city," or "U-City," in where major information systems (residential,

Experiencing art and culture as a lifestyle in subliminal harmony with the elements of nature, dreams and social interaction.

Credits: Jang Yoon Gyoo

medical, business, education, leisure) share data with computers are built into the houses, streets and office buildings that could yield unpredictable applications.

Extending the imagination a bit further is the Masdar City project- the most ambitious sustainable development initiative in the world today. When built, it will be the world's first zero carbon, zero waste city powered entirely by renewable energy sources taking living to a new level and will lead the world in understanding how all future cities should be built. This $20 billion project will be built in seven years located in Abu Dhabi linked to major destinations and businesses through a car-less, public transport system in conjunction with an innovative personal rapid transit system.

With architecture and new approach to commuting, communicating and sustaining growth on the rise, museums, science centers and exhibit environments and learning methodologies will undergo an unprecedented transformation at various levels. Flickr, Twitter, Blogs and Wikipedia phenomena are fueling a web-based highly interconnected complex social network of interactive and evolving dynamic dialogue. They are continuously seeking new definitions and paradigms of social culture. With Facebook crossing 100 million users in 2008 and YouTube logging 350 million monthly user-hits, the rising tide of shared learning is forcing museums to seek new perspectives on effective outreach beyond their walls. As the strategy shifts from technology laden living environments to inspirational buildings and cities in which technology enables personal lifestyle choices and corporate innovation, its impact will be felt in the way museums of the future will be conceived, built, used and remembered.

These transformative changes will invariably require an introspective adaptation for conventional training and currently offered academic programs in Museum Studies and Cultural Resource Management. Forces shaping and influencing the present and future of museum design are often external rather than from within the parentheisis of traditional museological discourses and practice. This could mean bringing on board an inter-disciplinary faculty into non-conventional and 'live' virtual class-room environments, infusing an element of engaging in the real and exploring the future in unpractised ways.

With cooperation, collaboration and collective sharing forming the vanguard of the new order of digital consumption, seeds of inspiration will continue to be sown by museum professionals and those associated directly or indirectly with heritage, learning and material culture. Every cyclical "seasonal" iteration will bring forth the blossoming of new ideas harvesting a new appreciation for the world we live in. ■

REFERENCES

Able, E. H. (1992). *International Partnerships*, Museum News, American Association of Museums.

Alembret, Bernadette. (1991). *A bridge between cultural communicator and curator*, MUSEUM Journal UNESCO: Vol.172, No.4.

Alexander, E.P. (1973). *Museums in Motion: An Introduction to the History and Functions of Museums*, American Association for State and Natural History, Nashville.

Appadurai, A. and Beckenridge, C.A. (1992). *Museums are Good to Think: Museums and Communities*, Editors Ivan Karp, C.M. Kreamer & S.D. Lavine; Smithsonian Institution Press.

Arnoldi, Mary-Jo.(1992). *A Distorted Mirror: The Exhibition of Herbert Ward Collection of Africana: Museums and Communities*, Smithsonian Institution Press.

Belcher, M. (1991). *Exhibitions in Museums*, Smithsonian Institution Press.

Berger, Craig and Skolnick, Lee (2007). *What is Exhibition Design?* Rotovision Press, Switzerland.

Bloom, Joel (1992). *Science & Technology Museums Face the Future- Museums and Public Understanding of Science*, Science Museum (London).

Lonnie, Bunch (1995). *Fighting the Good Fight: Museums in the Age of Uncertainty*, Museum News, American Association of Museums, Vol.74: No.2.

Cachia, F. (1987). *The Museum as a medium for Cross cultural Communication*, Museum Journal, UNESCO, No.153.

Cassar, M. (1995). *Environmental Management: Guidelines for Museums and Galleries*, Routlegde (NY).

Dana, J.C. (1999). *The New Museum: Selected Writings*, American Museums Association and Newark Museums Association.

Danilov, Victor J. (1982). *Science & Technology Centers*, MIT Press (MA).

Darragh, J. and Snyder J. S. (1993). *Museum Design: Planning and Building for the Arts*, Oxford University Press, American Federation for the Arts and The National Endowment for the Arts.

Dean, D. (1994) *Museum Exhibition: Theory and Practice*, Routledge (NY).

Decrosse, Ann and Landry, J. (1987). *Explora- The Permanent Exhibition of the Center for Science and Industry at La Villette, Paris*, Museum No.155.

Diamond, J. (1995). *Collaborative Multimedia*, CuratorVol.38, No.3.

Dison, M.E. (1996). *Taking cultural studies to the streets*, The Chronicle of Higher Education, Vol. XLII, No.20. A6.

Duitz, M. (1992). *The Soul of a Museum: Commitment to the community at Brooklyn Children's Museum, Museums and Communities*, Smithsonian Institution Press.

Falk, J.H. and Lynn D.D. (1992). *The Museum Experience*, Whalesback Books.

Fehrer, Elsa. (1993). *Learning Science with interactive Exhibits*, Curator, Col.36 No.4.

Finn, Bernard S. (1989). *The Museum of Science & Technology*, Museum Reference Guide, Greenwood Press.

Gawne, E. (1998). *Architects and Exhibition Design*, RIBA Heinz Gallery.

Geertz, C. (1973). *The Interpretation of Cultures*. Basic Books/ Harper Torch Books, NY.

Hall, J. (1992). *Arming for the Culture Wars,* Museum News, American Association of Museums.

Harris, M. (1981). *America Now: The Anthropology of a Changing Culture,* Touchstone, NY.

Hirzy, E.C. (1992). *Excellence Equity- Education and Public Dimensions of Museums.* American Association of Museums.

Jacob, George (1991). *Projects in Interactivity and Hypermedia in Museums: Problems and Opportunities,* Archives and Museum Informatics Technical Report, Pittsburgh.

Kahn, David. (1994). *Diversity and the Museum of London,* Curator, Museum Journal, Vol.34, No.4.

Kliment, S. (2001). *Building Type Basics for Museums,* John Wiley & Sons Inc. NY.

Lord, Gail Dexter and Barry (2001). *The Manual of Museum Exhibitions,* Altamira Press.

Nicholson, C. (1995). *Advisors to Partners: Bridging the Cultural Gap,* History News, Autumn.

Oppenheimer, Frank (1968). *A Rationale for Science Museum,* Curator, California Academy of Sciences, Vol.11.

Pegler, Martin (2002). *Contemporary Exhibit Design,* Harper-Collins Design.

Sudjic, Deyan. (2005). *The Edifice Complex,* Penguin Publications (London).

Swanson, T. (2005). *Space Odyssey- Making of a Visitor Experience at the Denver Museum of Nature and Science,* Museum Design Vo.1:1.

Tomislav, S. (1987). *The concept and nature of Museology,* Museum UNESCO, Vol.153.

Wheatley, Margaret J. (1992). *Leadership and the New Science,* Berret- Koehler Publishers Inc.

GEORGE JACOB

A former Smithsonian intern, George Jacob received his education at the Birla Institute of Technology & Science, University of Toronto and Yale School of Management, specializing in Museum Studies. A Canadian Commonwealth Scholar, he has worked on numerous museum projects spanning many countries, taught at various universities and has served on several professional Boards and Executive Councils. During his career spanning over two decades, he has been the founding Director of two science museums and has been an advocate of reform in the museum design-build industry. An artist, sculptor, thinker, writer, designer and master-planner, he continues to bring a confluence of talents to build institutional leadership and generate transformative change in the museum industry.

32161952R00140

Made in the USA
Charleston, SC
08 August 2014